TIME

DISASTERS
THAT SHOOK THE WORLD

Homecoming *In a disaster with a happy ending, the astronauts of the aborted Apollo 13 mission wait to board a rescue helicopter. They are aboard an inflatable raft after their command module made an emergency landing in the Pacific Ocean. The men survived a crisis in space after an explosion damaged their craft on its journey to the moon in 1970*

TIME

MANAGING EDITOR Richard Stengel
ART DIRECTOR D.W. Pine
DIRECTOR OF PHOTOGRAPHY Kira Pollack

Disasters That Shook the World

EDITOR Kelly Knauer
DESIGNER Ellen Fanning
PICTURE EDITOR Patricia Cadley
INTRODUCTION Amanda Ripley
RESEARCH Tresa McBee
COPY EDITOR Bruce Christopher Carr

TIME HOME ENTERTAINMENT INC.
PUBLISHER Richard Fraiman
VICE PRESIDENT, BUSINESS DEVELOPMENT AND STRATEGY Steven Sandonato
EXECUTIVE DIRECTOR, MARKETING SERVICES Carol Pittard
EXECUTIVE DIRECTOR, RETAIL AND SPECIAL SALES Tom Mifsud
EXECUTIVE DIRECTOR, NEW PRODUCT DEVELOPMENT Peter Harper
DIRECTOR, BOOKAZINE DEVELOPMENT AND MARKETING Laura Adam
PUBLISHING DIRECTOR Joy Butts
FINANCE DIRECTOR Glenn Buonocore
ASSISTANT GENERAL COUNSEL Helen Wan
ASSISTANT DIRECTOR, SPECIAL SALES Ilene Schreider
BOOK PRODUCTION MANAGER Suzanne Janso
DESIGN AND PREPRESS MANAGER Anne-Michelle Gallero
BRAND MANAGER Michela Wilde
ASSOCIATE PREPRESS MANAGER Alex Voznesenskiy

EDITORIAL DIRECTOR Stephen Koepp

SPECIAL THANKS
Christine Austin, Jeremy Biloon, Jim Childs, Susan Chodakiewicz, Rose Cirrincione, Lauren Hall Clark, Brian Fellows, Jacqueline Fitzgerald, Christine Font, Jenna Goldberg, Carrie Hertan, Hillary Hirsch, Amy Mangus, Robert Marasco, Kimberly Marshall, Amy Migliaccio, Nina Mistry, Dave Rozzelle, Adriana Tierno, TIME Imaging, Vanessa Wu

ISBN 10: 1-60320-247-1. ISBN 13: 978-1-60320-247-3. Library of Congress Control Number: 2011945982.

Published by TIME Books, an imprint of Time Home Entertainment Inc.
135 West 50th Street, New York, NY 10020

We welcome your comments and suggestions about TIME Books. Please write to us at:
TIME Books, Attention: Book Editors, P.O. Box 11016, Des Moines, IA 50336-1016

To order any of our hardcover Collector's Edition books, please call us at 1-800-327-6388.
Hours: Monday through Friday, 7 a.m.–8 p.m., or Saturday, 7 a.m.–6 p.m., Central Time

COVER PHOTO CREDITS
Front Cover: Great Chicago Fire: Currier & Ives—Library of Congress Prints and Photographs Division; *Titanic:* National Geographic Society—Corbis; *Costa Concordia:* Laura Lezza—Getty Images; *Challenger:* AP Images; Johnstown Flood: The Granger Collection; *Hindenburg:* Bettmann Corbis; Gulf oil slick: Daniel Beltra
Back Cover: Reno Air Races: Ward Howes—AP Images

ANDREAS SOLARO—AFP—GETTY IMAGES

Capsized *The cruise ship Costa Concordia ran aground off Italy's Giglio Island on Jan. 13, 2012*

Contents

Introduction

vi Surviving Disaster
Amanda Ripley, an authority on preparedness, explores the lessons we can learn from those who have weathered calamities

Disasters at Sea

4 Disaster on a Maiden Voyage
R.M.S. *Titanic* sinks after hitting an iceberg

16 From Legend to Reality
The remains of the *Titanic* are found in 1985

20 Great Lakes Mystery
The *Edmund Fitzgerald* is lost amid a mighty storm

22 Too Close to Shore
A luxury cruise liner sinks off Italy's coast in 2012

24 Deadly Shipwrecks
The stories behind the sinking of the Italian ocean liner *Andrea Doria* and two crowded excursion boats, the *General Slocum* and the *Eastland*

Disasters in the Air

28 Last Flight of the *Hindenburg*
The famed German zeppelin explodes while it is landing, ending the era of great airships

38 Future Imperfect
After the Concorde crashes on takeoff in 2000, the supersonic airliner is removed from service

40 Miracle on the Hudson
A steady captain guides a stricken jetliner to safety

42 Crash at an Air Show
Eleven spectators lose their lives when a World War II fighter smashes into a crowd in Nevada in 2011

44 Deadly Airplane Crashes
A tragedy in the Canary Islands, a mystery off Long Island, and a plane hits the Empire State Building

Disasters by Fire

48 Inferno in the Windy City
The Great Chicago Fire burned a quarter of the city

52 Tragedy in a Sweatshop
The Triangle Shirtwaist fire in 1911 leads to the passage of new laws to ensure workers' safety

56 Horror in Halifax
The explosion of a munitions ship lays waste to the graceful capital city of Nova Scotia

58 Stampede in a Nightclub
A fire at Boston's Cocoanut Grove kills 492 people

60 Tragedy Under the Big Top
A conflagration in a circus tent in 1944 kills 169 people, many of them women and children, in Hartford, Conn.

64 Deadly U.S. Fires
Disaster strikes at a rock club in Rhode Island, at a Las Vegas hotel and in a Chicago theater

Disasters in the Environment

68 Of Hurricanes and Humans
The flooding of New Orleans in 2005 was both a natural disaster and a failure of civil engineering

72 The Johnstown Flood
A Pennsylvania town is demolished after an artificial reservoir collapses and inundates a narrow valley

74 Fallacies and Fallout
A partial meltdown at the Three Mile Island plant shuts down the nuclear-power industry in the U.S.

76 Meltdown in Ukraine
A nuclear crisis at Chernobyl spreads radioactive fallout

80 Fukushima's Flaws
A huge tsunami in Japan unleashes a nuclear calamity

82 On the Rocks
The *Exxon Valdez* tanker hits a reef in Alaska in 1989, and leaking crude oil fouls a pristine natural setting

84 Oil Spill in the Gulf
An explosion at an oil rig imperils southern U.S. shores

86 Buried Alive
Thirty-three trapped miners are rescued in Chile in 2010

90 A Silent Cloud of Death
Leaking gas at a chemical plant in Bhopal, India, kills more than 15,000 people and injures many more

Disasters in Space

94 Farewell to the *Challenger*
A U.S. shuttle explodes on liftoff, and seven lives are lost

98 A Flawed Launch Leads to Disaster
The space shuttle *Columbia* breaks up on re-entry

102 Lost in Space
U.S. astronauts and engineers improvise an ingenious escape after an explosion during the Apollo 13 mission

106 Death on the Launchpad
Three U.S. astronauts die when fire strikes their capsule

Downfall *The airship Hindenburg crashes in flames as its hydrogen-filled internal cells explode at a New Jersey naval air station*

Surviving Disaster

By Amanda Ripley

To live fully is to live with an awareness
of the rumble of terror that underlies everything.
—ERNEST BECKER

HUMAN BEINGS HAVE COMPLICATED RELATIONships with modern disasters. We respond, first, by grieving for all that is lost. We pack up donations and write letters of profound compassion; we set up shrines and hot lines. Later, the relationship changes. We hold hearings to decide what went wrong and whom to blame. Much later, we visit the memorial and watch a film version, insulated by time from the horror.

As the years go by, we tell the stories of disasters again and again, shifting the focus slightly with each generation. In part, of course, we seek the simple thrill of being safely terrified (the same reason we buy tickets to watch zombies destroy the planet in 3-D). The frisson of brushing up against our own mortality never loses its fizz. But on some subconscious level perhaps, we also crave the opposite sensation. We deconstruct disasters to be assured of our own immortality. We lament the tragedy, shake our heads at the hubris that preceded it—and tell ourselves it could not happen again, not to us.

And yet, within all of us, there is a third, higher impulse. This impulse is to accept that horrific things can indeed happen to us—and then to try to learn from disasters in order to shift the odds, ever so slightly, in favor of a better world.

As a writer for TIME, I have been privileged to interview many disaster survivors over the years, and this is the one request I have heard from virtually all of them. Survivors want the rest of us to learn from what has happened—to make it worth something, despite everything. That is what careful histories of disasters, loyally told, can help us do.

This book, marking the 100th anniversary of the night the R.M.S. *Titanic* slipped bow-first into the sea, tells the stories of man-made disasters—complex fiascoes that, in most cases, were amplified by the technological wonders of the modern age. Notably, this volume also includes the stories of disasters that did not happen; tragedy averted can be just as important as tragedy realized. Through these stories we can recognize ourselves, our heroics and our flaws. We might reflect upon the everyday choices we make about where to live, what to protect and what not to worry about.

Because the truth is, disasters are getting more predictable, not less. Once upon a time, you could call a storm that killed hundreds of villagers a freak accident. But can you say the same when the storm was forecast for a week in advance of its arrival? When we had time to give it a name and order matching logowear for the TV reporter on the scene? "We know exactly—exactly—where the major disasters will occur," says Dennis Mileti, a sociologist who ran the Natural Hazards Center at the University of Colorado at Boulder for many years. "But individuals underperceive risk."

In A.D. 63, an earthquake seriously damaged the bustling city of Pompeii. The locals did not know that seismic tremors often go hand in hand with volcanic activity. And after the shaking stopped, they immediately went to work rebuilding, in the same spot—until a volcano buried them altogether 16 years later. Blind optimism has always been a charm and a curse. It's just getting harder to justify.

Today, about 91% of Americans live in places at a moderate-to-high risk of earthquakes, volcanoes, tornadoes, wildfires, hurricanes, flooding, high-wind damage or terrorism, according to an estimate calculated for TIME by the Hazards and Vulnerability Research Institute at the University of South Carolina. Very few of us will die in disasters, thankfully; but most of us will be affected by one. We can even predict what kind.

Wind and water are the mass-casualty perils we should fear the most. Of the more than 217 million people impacted by disasters globally in 2010, nearly 80% were affected by storms and floods, according to the Center for Research on the Epidemiology of Disasters. That's mostly because more of us live in dense, vertical cities near water than ever before. So the storms haven't changed much (not yet, anyway), but we have put more of our treasure in their paths.

The good news is that if we know which disasters to expect, we can do a better job preparing for them. We cannot prevent storms or shipwrecks, but we can minimize the odds that they will take hundreds of lives with them. After Hurricane Katrina, the Louisiana state legislature passed mandatory building codes (something Florida and other states had done years before). For every dollar spent on that kind of basic mitigation, society saves an average of $4, according to the nonprofit National Institute of Building Sciences.

Strikingly, we can even predict how we will behave in disasters. Whether we are in plane crashes or burning buildings, our brains tend to follow the same patterns. We know this because disaster survivors have told us so, again and again. First, most of us will experience a period of extreme disbelief. We will tell ourselves, despite the smoke curling across the ceiling or the water seeping in through the cabin door, that everything is fine. Captain Chesley ("Sully") Sullenberger deftly landed a jetliner in the Hudson River beside Manhattan in 2009. Afterward, he admitted that his first response to the sudden loss of thrust in both engines had been to normalize the situation. "My initial reaction was one of disbelief. 'I can't believe this is happening. This doesn't happen to me,'" he told Katie Couric in his first interview.

This is not necessarily bad news. Since we know that our first response to most disasters is to deny they are happening, we can follow the training given to pilots and flight attendants and take signs that something might be wrong seriously—worrying later about looking stupid. We can learn to override our urge to ignore fire alarms clanging late at night and, recalling fire victims everywhere, lead the way outside.

We can also predict what happens next. After the denial phase, most of us seek out other humans, including strangers. It happens deep underground in mining accidents and far out at sea. When people are told to leave before a hurricane or flood, most check with four or more sources—family, newscasters and officials, among others—before deciding what to do, sociologist Thomas Drabek has found. On 9/11, at least 70% of World Trade Center survivors talked with other people before trying to leave, according to the Federal Government's study of the evacuation.

We even know which of us will be the last to evacuate. In most disasters, including the nuclear accident at Three Mile Island, the elderly are the most resistant to leaving. Knowing that, we can go out of our way to talk to older neighbors before we leave town, and officials can design evacuation warnings specifically to appeal to someone who is 72.

After the deliberative phase, we act—or, more often than not, fail to act. The history of disasters proves that human beings very rarely panic in real life; to the contrary, we tend to become passive, obedient and sometimes even immobilized in all kinds of disasters. But we also know that if we

have engaged in some mental and physical rehearsal, giving our brain some memory of where the nearest exit is located or how a life jacket inflates, we can push through this instinct—just as Sully pushed past his disbelief.

All of this matters because we matter. As firefighters will tell you, the most important decisions in disasters are made by regular people, long before the ambulances arrive. In 1992, a series of sewer explosions caused by a gas leak ripped across Guadalajara, Mexico's second largest city. Starting at 10:30 a.m., at least nine separate underground blasts opened a jagged trench more than a mile long. Some 300 people died. The Mexican army was mobilized. Rescuers from California raced to help. Search-and-rescue dogs were called up. But first, before anyone else, regular people were on the scene helping one another. They lifted rubble off survivors with car jacks. They used garden hoses to force air into voids where people were trapped. Ordinary folks did the vast majority of rescues. After the first two hours, very few people were found alive. The search-and-rescue dogs arrived 24 hours later.

Since we know what kind of disasters will come to pass—and we even know how we will behave—the real question is, Why don't we make more out of this prescience? Why are more than half the buildings and homes in high-risk flood zones in the U.S. not protected by flood insurance? There are many good excuses, but it's fair to say that our handicaps are grounded in acquired ignorance and built-in bias. When it comes to many kinds of risks, we are born with a certain overconfidence, euphemistically called "optimism bias" by psychologists, and this arrogance often overtakes our reason. And in the U.S., our distrust of the government means that authorities must be sophisticated and creative to persuade us to prioritize risks and nudge us down a safer path.

But we can exploit our other strengths. We know, for example, that Americans share a cultural respect for self-sufficiency, for taking care of ourselves and our neighbors, without waiting for someone to protect us. That is a valuable asset we should redeploy, again and again. We also know that the brain prioritizes stories over statistics, and the more personalized the stories, the more powerful the imprint. So there is great practical value in telling stories, particularly when they are told with useful lessons attached.

In a media-saturated age, it's easy to mistake headlines for knowledge, to confuse tweets with insight. But there is a time for breaking news and a time for repairing what's broken. Learning from disasters means taking a deep breath, long after the satellite trucks have gone home—and reflecting on what we can do better. That is the ultimate tribute. ■

TIME *contributor Amanda Ripley is the author of* The Unthinkable: Who Survives When Disaster Strikes—and Why

Disasters
AT SEA

Battered *The ocean liner M.S.* Stockholm *arrives in New York City with its bow smashed in after its collision with the Italian Line ship* Andrea Doria *on July 25, 1956, off Nantucket Island.*

The Stockholm *was rebuilt and remains in service as M.S.* Athena. *The* Andrea Doria *sank, with the loss of 46 lives out of some 1,700 aboard the ship*

WHITE STAR LINE.

"OLYMPIC."
45,000 TONS.
AND
"TITANIC."
45,000 TONS.

THE LARGEST STEAMERS IN THE WORLD.

To NEW YORK,
From SOUTHAMPTON—CHERBOURG—QUEENSTOWN.
From LIVERPOOL—QUEENSTOWN.

To BOSTON,
From LIVERPOOL—QUEENSTOWN.

For Freight and Passage apply to

THOS. COOK & SON,

31, Fargate, SHEFFIELD;
16, Clumber Street and
97, Derby Road, NOTTINGHAM;
and Gallowtree Gate, LEICESTER.

Disaster on a Maiden Voyage

April 14-15, 1912

The luxurious ocean liner *Titanic* collides with an iceberg and sinks on its first journey

THE COLLISION SEEMED NOTHING MORE THAN A MILD JOLT, survivors later declared. It felt, said Lady Cosmo Duff Gordon, "as though somebody had drawn a giant finger along the side of the ship." The British fashion designer sat up in bed, but everything was quiet, so she lay back again. It was 11:40 p.m. local time in the North Atlantic Ocean some 400 miles (644 km) southeast of Newfoundland. Up in the first-class smoking room, where a group of young men were playing a last few rounds of cards, the grinding sound disturbed the game. Several of the players wandered out into the freezing night to take a look. "We hit an iceberg—there it is," somebody said. As the players looked toward the rear, they could see a dark mountain of ice receding into the distance. They went back to their game, and the White Star liner R.M.S. *Titanic* sailed majestically on.

The close encounter may have seemed only a glancing blow at first, but it soon proved deadly: within three hours *Titanic* would sink 12,500 ft. (3.8 km) to the bottom of the sea, claiming the lives of some 1,517 passengers and crew. The great ship was the most luxurious ocean liner yet built; promoted as "unsinkable," she was making her maiden voyage from Europe to the U.S. These compelling circumstances—the stark contrast between a great and ornate work of man, freshly launched, and the unexceptional

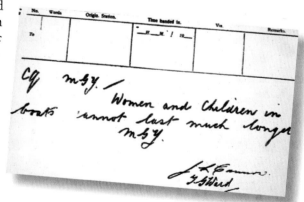

natural phenomenon that sent it to its doom—have conspired to make the fate of the *Titanic* the most celebrated of all man-made disasters.

As the world observes in April 2012 the centennial of the ship's sinking, the story of the *Titanic* and its demise continue to exert a powerful grip on the

Artifacts *At left, a White Star Line poster heralds the new* Titanic *and her sister ship,* Olympic. *Above, a handwritten draft of a radio message from the vessel*

5

human imagination. There are two *Titanics,* it seems: the real ship that sank a century ago, and its doppelgänger, the doomed vessel of myth and legend, stage and screen, its tale told anew in every generation. When the story was still fresh, books of survivors' stories and recountings of the wreck were consistent best sellers. Before the year 1912 was out, two films had already been made about the tragedy, one starring survivor Dorothy Gibson; other films based on the tale appeared in 1929, 1943 and 1953. In 1915 Thomas Hardy's powerful poem *The Convergence of the Twain* posited the sinking of the ship as a deadly lesson in the dominance of nature over the works of man.

In 1955 writer Walter Lord's detailed account of the wreck, *A Night to Remember,* topped the best-seller lists for months; Hollywood's version followed in 1958. *The Unsinkable Molly Brown,* a musical comedy based on the story of a famous survivor, debuted in 1960; a movie version appeared four years later.

In 1985 the tale of the *Titanic* once again made headlines around the world—and the cover of TIME—when a multinational team of explorers announced they had located the remains of the ship on the ocean floor. In the years that followed, *Titanic* fever was everywhere, as fascinating images of the wreckage of the luxury liner thrilled and intrigued viewers in publications around the world and on the oversized IMAX movie screen.

The fever crested in 1997, when a new Broadway musical account of the tale won five Tonys, including Best Musical. But that version's impact was dwarfed by movie director James Cameron's lavish 3-hr. film of the story, which became one of the biggest hits in Hollywood history, earning $1.8 billion and making major stars of its two young leading actors, Leonardo DiCaprio and Kate Winslet. The film, with its remarkable depiction of the sinking of the ship, is slated to be released in a new, 3-D format in time for the centennial of the catastrophe.

Larger than life from its launch, *Titanic* was making news well before she sank. In an era when grandiose ocean liners were the subject of awe and admiration, she was the biggest passenger ship ever built, designed to be a magnet for the wealthy and a marvel for the general public. On her maiden voyage, her decks were heavy with millionaires, occupying suites that cost $2,300 to $4,350 (roughly $52,000 to $99,000 in 2012 terms) apiece. Among the first-class passengers sauntering aboard for her maiden voyage were a dozen great names familiar from U.S. society pages, including John Jacob Astor IV, whose net worth was some $125 million; George Widener, heir to a fortune worth $30 to 50 million; and Benjamin Guggenheim, with around $95 million.

Here was a world of Beaux Arts luxury: cigars and astra-

A majestic passage
Nuzzled by assisting tugboats, Titanic *departs Southampton, England, on April 10, bound for Cherbourg, France*

All aboard! *An excited crowd awaits the arrival of* Titanic *in Queenstown, Ireland, on April 11, where 130 new passengers came aboard on the ship's last stop before its transatlantic crossing. The ship was built in Belfast by the firm of Harland & Wolff*

khan coats, Burgundy and champagne, women gliding in extravagant gowns amid elegant furnishings. And miraculously, thanks to the ship's owners, the White Star Line, that world was afloat. Everyone was sure that, like the age she symbolized, the *Titanic* would last forever. Instead, her demise wrote an emphatic ending to this period of cocky opulence, especially when viewed in hindsight. In fewer than three years, World War I would begin, and the era of Edwardian splendor would likewise sink, slipping beneath the mud in the trenches of France and Belgium.

On the sea, size matters—and *Titanic* was enormous. The great ship weighed 46,328 gross tons and was 882.5 ft. (269 m) long; imagine a craft as lengthy as three football fields, or roughly 3½ city blocks, steaming serenely through the waves, the largest man-made moving object on the planet. Her two reciprocating engines, plus a newfangled low-pressure turbine engine, devoured 650 tons

of coal a day and could drive the *Titanic* at a speed of up to 23 knots. To earn her reputation as "unsinkable," the ship had a double bottom and 16 watertight compartments in her hull. Mrs. Albert Caldwell, a survivor, later remembered that she had asked one of the deckhands whether the *Titanic* was truly unsinkable. "Yes, lady," he had said. "God himself could not sink this ship."

With that air of invincibility, the *Titanic* set forth on her maiden voyage on April 10, 1912. Her route was from Southampton, England, to Cherbourg, France; Queenstown, Ireland; and New York City. Few noticed that her builders, while lavishing money on luxuries, had scrimped when it came to emergencies: the big ship carried 2,227 people—and lifeboats for only 1,178 of them.

The mighty liner departed Ireland on schedule, on the afternoon of Thursday, April 11, and enjoyed an unevent-

Constitutionals *Passengers stroll on the ship's second-class promenade. Some of the photographs of life aboard the ship were taken by amateur photographers who disembarked before the luxury liner left Ireland for the U.S.*

ful passage for the next three days. She was due to arrive in New York City on the 16th, and the night of the 15th would be reserved for packing for arrival. As a result, Sunday, April 14, was designated the voyage's formal night, and the ship—whose vertical layout reflected the period's social order—was lively and loud all evening. Up top, first-class passengers donned their most splendid attire for a formal dinner hosted by Captain Edward J. Smith. Second-class travelers celebrated in more restrained fashion: about 100 of them gathered to sing hymns in their Dining Saloon. Things were rowdier below, in the third-class sec-

Things were rowdier below, in the third-class section, where a spirited dance was taking place

tion of the ship, where a spirited dance was taking place.

Even as the passengers sang and sashayed, the ship was heading directly for a great field of icebergs. It was a cold, clear night on the North Atlantic, and there was no moon, diminishing visibility. Later inquiries showed that *Titanic* received six messages on April 14 warning of the approaching ice field—but they were all disregarded. About 11 p.m., the radio operator of a ship traveling not far ahead of *Titanic,* the *Californian,* violated protocol by breaking into *Titanic's* outgoing broadcast to report it was surrounded by icebergs. The luxury liner's radio operator berated his counterpart for the interruption and did not pass the message along.

Some 40 minutes later, a lookout in *Titanic's* crow's nest—who did not have binoculars, due to a minor miscue—saw a large iceberg dead ahead of the ship and delivered a double warning, ringing the lookout bell three

Sweeping ascent *A marvel in wood and wrought iron, the Grand Staircase was the centerpiece of the ship's internal design for its wealthiest passengers. Located under an expansive, white-enameled skylight, it was a primary vertical passage through the ship's four top decks for first-class travelers, connecting the promenade on A Deck to the Dining Saloon on D Deck*

times and telephoning the bridge, where First Officer William McMaster Murdoch immediately ordered the crew to reverse engines and turn to port. As the big mass of ice slid by on the ship's starboard side, the lookouts realized why they had not seen it sooner: it was a "blue 'berg," one that had just turned upside down in the water and thus was wet and unusually dark.

The collision with the iceberg (latitude 41° 46 min. N., longitude 50° 14 min. W.) occurred at 11:40 p.m. At first the crew thought no damage had been done, and few passengers realized that anything had happened. Chief night baker Walter Belford was in the galley making rolls for the following day; the slight jolt of the collision caused a pan of them to clatter to the floor. But a steerage passenger named Carl Johnson found his shoes underwater when he tried to get dressed, and Mrs. Henry B. Harris, wife of a theatrical producer, noticed that the dresses

which had been gently swaying in her closet suddenly stopped swaying. Mrs. Arthur Ryerson, a steel heiress, asked a steward what was the matter. "There's talk of an iceberg, ma'am," he replied.

Titanic was built to remain afloat if as many as four of her watertight compartments were flooded. But the irregular series of gashes in her hull inundated five compartments. Down below, water began pouring into the mail room, swirling knee deep around workers as they tried to haul sacks of mail to a higher deck. When word of the leaks reached the bridge, somebody asked Captain Smith whether he thought the ship was seriously damaged. He paused, then slowly said, "I'm afraid she is."

Confronting the unthinkable, Captain Smith had to move gradually from disbelief to doubt to desperation. It was 12:05 a.m. when he ordered all passengers mustered on deck, 12:15 when the first call for help was sent out on

Working out *Ship's trainer T.W. McCawley shows off a rowing machine in the gymnasium; behind him, electrician William Parr bestrides a "mechanical camel" apparatus*

Lap of luxury *Among the ship's grandest amenities was the opulent Turkish Bath, a large suite with a steam room, hot room, temperate room, shampoo room and cooling room*

Bon appétit! *With large windows overlooking the sea, the Café Parisien was a popular innovation for first-class passengers, evoking the atmosphere of a sidewalk café*

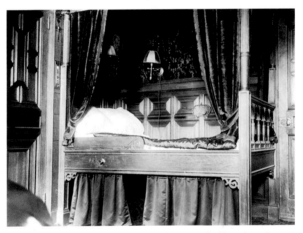

Sweet dreams *This first-class parlor suite, half-timbered in a mock-Tudor style, was one of several luxury suites that included a number of rooms in distinct period décors*

Officers *Purser Hugh Walter McElroy, left, poses with Captain Edward J. Smith. After supervising the boarding of the lifeboats, the men perished when the ship went down*

Old and new *The first-class reading room was decorated in a Georgian style, but the ship also boasted up-to-date electrical appliances: telephones, heaters and table fans*

THE NEW YORK HERALD.

THE TITANIC SINKS WITH 1,800 ON BOARD; ONLY 675, MOSTLY WOMEN AND CHILDREN, SAVED

MOST APPALLING DISASTER IN MARINE HISTORY OCCURS WHEN WORLD'S LARGEST STEAMSHIP STRIKES GIGANTIC ICEBERG AT NIGHT

Headlines *News of* Titanic's *fate arrived in New York City early on the morning of April 15. Throughout the day, large crowds gathered at the White Star Line offices and outside newspaper buildings to read the latest dispatches about the catastrophe.*

In the illustration at top, the doomed ship, its bow underwater, is beginning to break apart as it sinks

the wireless, 12:45 when the first lifeboats were lowered. Occupancy followed the ancient code of the sea: women and children first. First-class passengers were closer to the lifeboats and so, while almost all the women in first class escaped, more than half of those in third class drowned. Accounts stating that the ship's crew barred third-class passengers from entering the lifeboats are unfounded. Historian Lord, who researched his detailed account of the sinking, *A Night to Remember,* for 28 years and conducted scores of interviews with survivors, once noted that, when asked how they left the ship, "nearly every woman survivor replied firmly, 'In the last boat.'"

Some men took seats. Bruce Ismay, managing director of the White Star Line, was among them; he was later denounced as a coward and lived his remaining years in shamed seclusion. Amid the haste, errors were made. Lifeboat 1, which could have held 40 people, departed with only twelve aboard. At 2:05 a.m., Captain Smith went into the wireless shack for the last time and said, "Men, you have done your full duty. You can do no more. Abandon your cabin. Now it's every man for himself."

There was genuine heroism in the ship's last moments afloat. *Titanic's* orchestra kept playing, in a wonderful gesture of valor. Mrs. Isidor Straus stepped from the gunwale of a boat back onto the deck to share death with her beloved financier husband, co-owner of Macy's depart-

Rescue *Above, survivors in* Titanic *lifeboats approach the* Carpathia *liner and are brought aboard in the early-morning hours after* Titanic *sank, around 2:20 a.m.* Titanic *did not carry enough lifeboats to save all aboard, although it met badly outdated British safety codes. This failure—and the belief that the ship was "unsinkable"—explains why more than half the passengers died at sea. Below, survivors survey ice floes from* Carpathia's *deck*

ment store. "Where you go, I go," she said, and they sat down together in a couple of deck chairs. A gallant Southerner, Major Archie Butt, military aide to President William H. Taft, went to his death as he courteously bowed women into the boats.

Even as the ship began listing to port, rescue efforts had begun. *Titanic* sent its first Mayday signal just after midnight, and it began firing white skyrockets, a standard distress signal. The nearest ship was the *Californian,* only some 10 miles (16 km) ahead of *Titanic,* but the ship's captain ignored the liner's appeals. Instead, it was the *Carpathia,* a smallish Cunard Line ship, 58 miles (93 km) east of *Titanic,* that responded to her pleas; Captain Arthur H. Rostron reversed *Carpathia's* course and sent her plowing, full speed ahead, toward the sinking vessel.

Titanic's bow, her front section, flooded first, as seawater flowed into the forward hatches; when its stern began to rise, every movable item on the ship plunged forward, into the bow. Most of the lifeboats were now in the water, and passengers were being swept into the sea, in whose 28° waters most people could not survive longer than 20 minutes. As seawater flooded into the ship, its lights suddenly went dark. The stern rose higher and higher, with passengers clinging to every available surface as the bow began to dip beneath the waves and the ship's funnels began crashing down. As Daniel Butler reports in his thorough 1998 book, *Unsinkable,* Second Officer Charles H. Lightoller, manning a collapsible lifeboat, "heard a sound that would haunt him for the rest of his life: as the ship began her final plunge, he could hear people—husbands and wives, brothers and sisters, parents and children—crying out to each other: 'I love you.'"

The waters soon closed over the ship's stern; as it sank beneath the waves, it broke completely in two. Some 7½ min. after *Titanic* plunged below the surface of the sea, its two sections plowed into the ocean floor. About two hours later, the *Carpathia* arrived on the scene and began retrieving the chilled survivors from a calm sea.

Titanic had sunk. The great ship was dead, but its second life was just beginning. In the decades to come, the stories of her doomed maiden voyage—and theories about the circumstances that sank her—would proliferate. Only a few dreamers imagined that human eyes would ever gaze again upon the great liner. But 73 years later, in 1985, a team of veteran explorers located the lost legend. ■

The Survivors

■ Of the 2,200 people believed to be aboard the *Titanic*, 1,517 perished and more than 700 survived. A number of the ship's officers, following standard procedure for emergencies, took command of lifeboats to ensure the passengers would be picked up safely, and thus survived to become key eyewitnesses to the sinking.

The most senior crew member to survive was Second Officer Charles H. Lightoller, who directed the boarding of the lifeboats on the port side of the ship. Swept into the sea as the ship went down, he was almost pulled under by the vortex created by the sinking vessel, but a blast of hot air from a ventilator drove him back to the surface. He later provided testimony about *Titanic's* last moments before committees of inquiry in both Britain and the U.S.

MOLLY BROWN Born Margaret Tobin to Irish immigrants in Missouri, she gloried in her humble origins after she married "Leadville Johnny" Brown, who struck it rich with a gold mine. The most charismatic survivor was christened "The Unsinkable Molly Brown," and her story was celebrated in a Broadway musical of that name, which later became a film starring Debbie Reynolds.

HAROLD BRIDE The ship's junior wireless operator manned the telegraph after the crash, sending out the then-new distress signal, SOS. Swept off the ship while helping deploy a collapsible life boat, he survived; below, he is carried off the *Carpathia*. He was an eyewitness to the ship's last moments.

Read all about it *Hawking one of the great stories of the 20th century, on April 16 newspaper boy Ned Parfett sells copies of the* Evening News *telling of* Titanic's *maritime disaster outside the White Star Line offices on London's Cockspur Street*

THE ASTORS Scion of a great New York City family, John Jacob Astor IV was the wealthiest person aboard *Titanic*. The inventor and Spanish-American War veteran had shocked society by divorcing his first wife to marry, at 47, the 18-year-old Madeleine Talmage Force. After the collision, Astor cut apart a life jacket to demonstrate its operation to his wife, then placed her, as well as a maid and a nurse, aboard a lifeboat. He asked to join his pregnant wife on a lifeboat, but did not argue when he was denied a seat.

DOUGLAS SPEDDEN The young man, child of a well-to-do New York State family, was only 6 when he boarded *Titanic*. Awakened after the crash, he was put in Lifeboat 3 with his mother and slept through most of the night, waking at dawn to marvel at a nearby iceberg. Only three years later, the young *Titanic* survivor died after running into a street to chase a football and being hit by a car.

MILLVINA DEAN Shown above in her mother Georgetta's arms, Dean was the youngest person aboard the ship; the third-class passenger was only 9 weeks old on *Titanic's* maiden voyage. She became the last survivor of the shipwreck to die, passing away at age 97 on May 31, 2009—the 98th anniversary of *Titanic's* launch at the Harland & Wolff shipyard in Belfast.

From Legend To Reality

September 1, 1985

The remains of *Titanic* provide new clues as to how the great ship sank

T HE DYNAMICS OF MYTHOLOGY GENERALLY FLOW in only one direction: be it the assassination of a President, the acts of rebellion that kindled a revolution or the backstage doings of rock stars, the unvarnished facts, over time, become burnished with the sheen of fiction. But in 1985 the world woke up one day to find a modern myth, long since consigned to murky legend, swimming into sudden focus as tangible, photographable reality: 12,500 ft. (38,100 m) beneath the surface of the sea, the doomed ship *Titanic* had been found. As they gazed at photographs of the sunken leviathan, millions of people around the world, for the first time, could sense her mass, her eerie quiet and the ruined splendor of a lost age.

Here were the artifacts of extravagance, as flawlessly preserved as those in the tomb of King Tutankhamun. Five cases of wine with corks seemingly intact. Delicate china plates, wash basins and chamber pots, pristine and unchipped. Plump and elegant luggage that could have been packed yesterday. The luxury liner had been found in two parts, both sitting nearly upright on the frigid Atlantic floor, 400 miles (644 km) south of Newfoundland. At that depth, the great ship and its trove of relics had been shielded from the destructive effects of sunlight, heat, algae and parasites. For millions, the unexpected reappearance of the Edwardian-era ship was a welcome touch of vintage nostalgia, like the sight of a top hat or a long white glove.

Robert Ballard, a former U.S. Navy captain and veteran Woods Hole Oceanographic Institution scientist, had long wanted to find the wreck, first attempting the feat in 1977, to no avail. It wasn't until 1985 that he would find a way to finance his research. Ballard approached the Navy for funding, which he secured on the condition of locating two sunken Navy submarines—the U.S.S. *Thresher* and U.S.S. *Scorpion,* both cold war–era nuclear submarines—lost some years before. He was required to first find the submarines on the sea floor and photograph them (a secret mission that Ballard didn't reveal until 2008) before using a pair of unmanned underwater robots to search for *Titanic.* In the early hours of Sept. 1, Ballard, in conjunction with a French expedition, tracked a debris trail to the ship's remains. Video and pho-

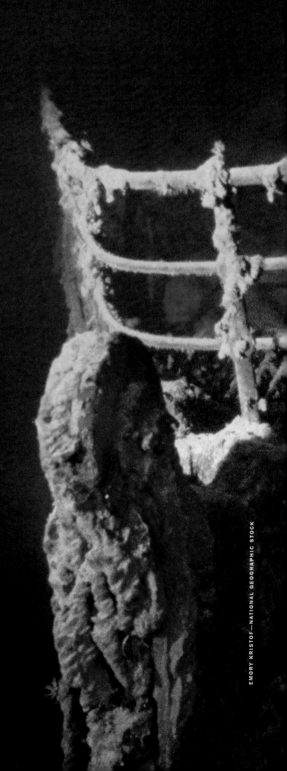

tographs were taken and later broadcast to a surprised, then exhilarated and astonished, world.

A year after the remains of the ship were discovered, Ballard and other oceanographers returned to the site to explore the sections of the ship's bow and stern and the extensive debris field that lay between the two. They compiled 60 hr. of video and 60,000 stills garnered during the 12-day exploration by the manned submersible *Alvin,* the remotely operated vehicle J.J. and the towed sled Angus. The new trove of details turned what had at first seemed an exercise in legend and romance into a new chapter in the scientific study of *Titanic's* fate.

Ballard's deep-diving craft failed to find the 300-ft. (91.5 m) gash that, according to legend, was torn in the *Titanic's* hull when its starboard side collided with the iceberg. Instead, he suggested, the collision had buckled the ship's plates, allowing water to pour in. The expedition also brought back evidence that the ship broke apart not when she hit bottom, as he had thought when viewing the first *Titanic* images in 1985, but as she sank: the stern, which settled on the bottom almost 1,800 ft. (549 m) from the bow, had swiveled 180 degrees on its way down.

Soon other scientists and corporations began to visit the ruins of the ship, ownership of which was the subject of some dispute. Finally, in 1994, the company RMS Titanic Inc. (formed by Premier Exhibitions, which designs museum exhibitions and maintains artifacts) was named salvor-in-possession of the wreck, gaining the rights to collect found artifacts and launch expeditions to the ship. In a series of seven visits to the wreck, the firm collected more than 5,500 artifacts, ranging from china dishes to leather trunks filled with preserved bank notes.

The ongoing series of expeditions has attracted more than a few critics. Many argue that collecting items from the wreckage violates a sacred resting ground. Ballard agrees: he has insisted repeatedly that the remains should be left undisturbed. After his 1985 discovery, he remarked, "The ship is in beautiful condition where it is. I am opposed to the desecration of this memorial to 1,500 souls."

Others argue that all the disturbances are causing the

Stirring *A retrieved teaspoon bears the name of the ship as its handle, while the bowl carries an etching of the vessel*

ship to deteriorate faster than it would if left alone. But those same expeditions have dispelled some of the myths surrounding the sinking, and two recent books have advanced fresh theories about the fate of the big liner.

In their 2008 book, *What Really Sank the Titanic: New Forensic Discoveries,* scientists Jennifer Hooper McCarty and Tim Foecke, noting Ballard's discovery that the hull simply collapsed in places, argue that the steel used in the hull wasn't weak, as some had suspected. After studying rivets retrieved from the wreckage, they identified these critical iron pins, which held the exterior steel hull plates together, as the culprits. Belfast builders Harland & Wolff, they posited, were under great pressure from an overloaded building schedule and resorted to using second-rate iron rivets, which easily shattered when the ship hit the iceberg. The company, unsurprisingly, strongly disputes that claim.

In another 2008 book, *Titanic's Last Secrets,* writer Bradford Matsen reported on the work of wreck-diving historians Richie Kohler and John Chatterton, who argue that two recently discovered pieces of the *Titanic's* bottom prove the ship's stern did not rise high in the air before sinking, as portrayed in James Cameron's 1997 film *Titanic,* where the stern is almost perpendicular to the water. They also take issue with Ballard's 1986 argument that the ship broke in two after it sank: they believe the ship broke up and sank while still relatively flat on the surface. Survivors' testimony, maddeningly, can be used to support either view. The larger fact remains: there is much for science yet to discover from the shipwreck.

In 2010, a new era in *Titanic* studies was launched, when a team of Woods Hole scientists began creating a "virtual *Titanic,*" a digital 3-D map created by imaging technology carried aboard submersible craft, that will allow not only scientists but anyone else on the planet who has access to the Internet to explore the *Titanic* in 3-D, without submersibles, intermediaries—or danger. ∎

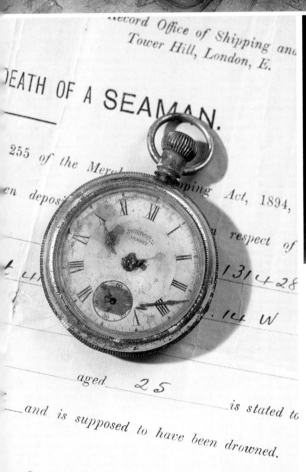

1

2

3

DEATH OF A SEAMAN.

Record Office of Shipping and
Tower Hill, London, E.

255 of the Mer... ...ping Act, 1894,

...en deposit... ...n respect of

...131 28

...14 W

aged 25

...is stated to

...and is supposed to have been drowned.

7

Remains *Visits to the wreck have revealed a stunning array of artifacts, many of them very well preserved:*
1. *Steering wheel*
2. *Starboard propeller*
3. *China plates*
4. *Winches for mast*
5. *Stateroom*
6. *Iron deck bench*
7. *Timepiece*

4

6

5

Great Lakes Mystery

November 10, 1975

What caused the wreck of the *Edmund Fitzgerald?*

THE LEGEND LIVES ON, FROM THE CHIPPEWA on down, of the big lake they call Gitche Gumee. Lake Superior, it is said, presents the most danger to the hundreds of freighters that ply its waters in early November, when Arctic winds whip across its waters. It was on such a November night in 1975 that the greatest freighter on the Great Lakes, the S.S. *Edmund Fitzgerald,* went down amid heavy seas. All 29 hands aboard drowned, as immortalized in Gordon Lightfoot's 1976 ballad *The Wreck of the Edmund Fitzgerald.*

Launched in 1958, the *Fitzgerald* was a cut above other freighters on Lake Superior. Built to just clear the locks of the St. Lawrence Seaway, it was 729 ft. (222 m) long, 75 ft. (23 m) across the beam and 39 ft. (12 m) deep. Its bridge, common rooms and lounges were lavish by Great Lakes standards. But impressive as it seemed to sailors,

the big freighter was battered and limping on the afternoon of Nov. 10, 1975, as it was southbound from northern Wisconsin to the Detroit area. A big gale was roiling the chilly waters of Superior, creating 10-ft. (3 m) waves that crashed over the ship's long top deck, beneath which it held some 26,116 tons of taconite pellets.

For safety's sake, the *Fitzgerald* was traveling roughly in tandem with another freighter, the S.S. *Arthur M. Anderson.* Late in the afternoon, the *Anderson* was registering winds of 58 knots (67 m.p.h., or 107 km/h). Amid the gale, Captain Ernest McSorley of the *Fitzgerald,* some 10 miles (16 km) ahead of the *Anderson,* advised the other freighter that his ship had lost both radar systems, had sustained damage to its topside and was taking on water with its bilge pumps running. Effectively blind, McSorley asked the *Anderson* to help it navigate the storm, and the *Ander-*

Memorial *The Split Rock Lighthouse beacon on the coast of Lake Superior in Minnesota, now decomissisoned, is lit up each year on Nov. 10 to commemorate the sinking of the* Edmund Fitzgerald. *At far left is the ship; its bell was recovered in 1995*

son moved closer to do so. At 7:10 p.m., McSorley sent the last communication from the *Edmund Fitzgerald*: "We are holding our own."

But the big freighter wasn't holding its own: it disappeared from the *Anderson's* radar screens fewer than 10 minutes later. The *Anderson,* other nearby ships and search aircraft swept the area throughout the night and for the next few days, but no survivors were found.

Why did the *Fitzgerald* sink? The U.S. Coast Guard suggested in 1977 that faulty hatch closures were to blame, but this explanation was doubted by many. Others pointed to a long-rumored phenomenon of the lake, a set of three enormous waves, the "three sisters," said to have beset other ships. As TIME's Bryan Walsh reported in 2010, scientists now believe such "rogue waves"—sudden huge waves that can emerge out of the open water with-

out warning—are a reality rather than mariners' legend.

In 1995, an oil rig in the North Sea recorded an 84-ft. (25.6 m) -high wave that appeared out of nowhere, and in 2000, a British oceanographic vessel recorded a 95-ft. (29 m) -high wave off the coast of Scotland. On March 3, 2010, a sudden wall of water hit a luxury cruise ship sailing off Spain in the Mediterranean Sea, killing two people and injuring 14. At this time, scientists cannot explain the origin of these monster walls of water.

The wreck of the *Fitzgerald* was located in 1976 and it has been probed several times by divers. In 1995, the ship's bell, heavily corroded, was brought to the surface and restored to gleaming beauty; it can be seen at the Great Lakes Shipwreck Museum at Whitefish Point, Mich. A new bell was placed at the wreck; it bears the names of the 29 sailors who died on that dread November evening ∎

Too Close To Shore

January 13, 2012

A cruise ship runs aground and capsizes off the Italian coast

Under fire *Captain Schettino, above, was widely criticized for his handling of the accident, which left the* Costa Concordia *aground just off the shore of Giglio Island*

Dissasters are most distressing when they are entirely avoidable. And though it was too early as this book went to press for a final judgment to be rendered in the case of the *Costa Concordia,* the Italian cruise ship that ran aground on Friday, Jan. 13, off the shore of Giglio Island in the Tyrrhenian Sea along Italy's west coast, there was every indication that the tragedy should never have occurred.

The luxury liner, owned by Costa Crociere, a unit of Carnival Corp., was on a weeklong cruise of the western Mediterranean, idling along the scenic coast about 9:45 p.m. The late-dinner service had just begun in the main dining room, when, as Sicilian native Alessandra Grasso, 24, told the New York *Times:* "In a moment, everything was up in the air. People, chairs, glasses, food."

The 1,017 ft. (310 m) -long ship, a floating resort with some 4,200 passengers and crew onboard, was passing between the Italian coast and Giglio, a popular tourist island 18 mi. (29 km) offshore, rather than in the open sea on the far side of the island, as called for in its approved itinerary. It had struck a submerged reef or rock, tearing a 160-ft. (49 m) gash in its hull. In the moments that followed, the ship's loudspeakers announced a power outage and urged those aboard to remain calm. According to one passenger, dinner waiters told patrons to remain seated even as the ship began badly listing. Twenty minutes later, the order to abandon ship was issued, causing panic and a stampede in the direction of the lifeboats.

Passengers described a nightmarish scene, which many compared to the movie *Titanic,* as they swarmed, crawled and slid through the listing ship's corridors, trying to reach safety. Some threw themselves into the sea, whose waters were a frigid 57°F (14°C) and swam their way to shore, a distance of about 400 ft. (122 m). Others clam-

bered down ladders into lifeboats, only to find the crew members in charge of the emergency craft were untrained and inept. "The pilots were not sailors but waiters who had no idea how to maneuver and kept on having us turning in circles," reported Giancarlo Sammatrice, 22, a vacationing cook from Sicily. An evacuation drill had been scheduled for the next day, cruise line officials said.

Amid the chaos, Captain Francesco Schettino, 52, abandoned ship in a lifeboat well before all passengers were accounted for. Within days, Italian newspapers published transcripts of a phone conversation between Schettino and an angry Livorno Port Authority chief Gregorio De Falco, who berated the captain and ordered him to return

to the ship and determine the status of the passengers. Schettino reluctantly agreed to do so, but apparently never did. He was questioned by local police, then detained and finally put under house arrest. Cruise line executives, who had initally defended the crew, soon reversed course and implicated the captain. "I can't deny there was human error," said Costa Crociere CEO Pier Luigi Foschi. "We're talking about an initiative that commander Schettino took, according to his own will and contrary to our rules of conduct." The captain reportedly claimed that the cruise line sanctioned the maneuver. Either way, the unplanned close approach appears to have been designed to offer viewers on Giglio a close encounter with the daz-zling, enormous *Costa Concordia.* In a word: showboating.

As divers and rescue workers scoured the ship for survivors, they eventually blew holes in its hull to provide access to submerged areas. As of Jan. 27, the death toll stood at 16, and Italian authorities said that some 20 passengers were still unaccounted for. Meanwhile, choppy seas and high winds were shifting the capsized ship's position, leading to concerns that the 500,000 gallons of fuel in its tanks might leak, polluting the sea and coast. As rescue workers fought the elements, hoping to recover bodies and head off an environmental disaster, the world's cruise ship lines, their safety policies now under a microscope, were also bracing for rough weather ahead. ■

Deadly Shipwrecks
Time has eroded the memory of some maritime disasters

July 25, 1956
Last Hours of the *Andrea Doria*

Named for a great Renaissance admiral, S.S. *Andrea Doria* was the pride of the Italian Line fleet after its launch in 1951. But in July 1956, bound from Genoa to New York City amid heavy fog, the ship collided with a Swedish ocean liner, M.S. *Stockholm,* off Nantucket Island. Fortunately, a strong relief effort managed to remove most passengers from the stricken vessel, which stayed afloat, slowly subsiding into the waves, for about 11 hours after the crash.

Of some 1,700 aboard the *Andrea Doria,* 46 died, as well as five of *Stockholm's* crew. The two cruise lines settled out of court, so there was no official determination of blame for the crash. The sinking of the ship, below, was closely documented by news media.

July 24, 1915
Tragedy in Slow Motion

As hundreds of Czech immigrants bound for a company picnic in Michigan City, Ind., boarded the excursion boat S.S. *Eastland* early on a July morning at its pier in downtown Chicago, the ship began to list heavily to port. Launched in 1903 and originally designed to haul produce, the "Speed Queen of the Great Lakes" had proved to be top-heavy and susceptible to listing, and when it was redesigned to serve as an excursion vessel that could carry more than 2,500 passengers, it became even less seaworthy. A federal safety measure instituted after the 1912 sinking of the *Titanic*—the addition of enough heavy lifeboats to carry all aboard to safety in an emergency—only added to the ship's off-kilter tendencies.

After listing dangerously for several minutes, the crowded ship rolled over completely at 7:28 a.m. There were few theatrics or hero-ics: one eyewitness declared the ship simply rolled over on its side "as slowly as an egg boiling in water." Many passengers survived, clambering on to the ship's hull, above, then to the deck of a nearby tugboat and onto the wharf. But 844 of the estimated 2,572 on the ship drowned in the second deadliest marine disaster in U.S. history.

FIVE MEMBERS OF THE OELLRICH FAMILY OF BROOKLYN, LOST IN THE DISASTER.

The Father, William Oellrich, Survives, as Does the Boy Henry, Aged 11, Shown Standing in the Picture. The Mother, Annie, and the Two Little Ones in the Picture Are Missing, as Well as Two Other Children.

LIST OF SLOCUM'S DEAD NOW MAY REACH 1,000

June 15, 1904

Panic on a Picnic Cruise

By all accounts, the June day set aside for the annual excursion of the Sunday school of St. Mark's Evangelical Lutheran Church in Manhattan was bright and lovely. On a pier in the East River, some 1,331 people, mainly German-American mothers and children, boarded a sidewheel steamboat, the *General Slocum,* heading for a picnic on the North Shore of Long Island. The ship's band was playing *A Mighty Fortress Is Our God* as, amid a jangle of bells and a fountain of spray, Captain William Van Schaick, 67, ordered the *General Slocum* to embark a little after 9 a.m. A deckhand soon noticed that a small fire was burning brightly on a storeroom floor. Suddenly, flowers of flame were growing through the ship's decks, sprouting in the passageways, streaming out of the portholes. Passengers panicked as they discovered that all the life preservers were full of dust, not cork, while the ship's useless lifeboats sank when they were launched. Few Americans could swim in those days, and as many women and girls leaped into the water to avoid the flames, the voluminous skirts of the era dragged them to their deaths.

Captain Van Schaick may have panicked as well; he steered his burning boat past several nearby shores before he finally beached it on North Brother Island, where he fled the ship and survived. He was later convicted of negligence and served a jail term. Above, only the ship's steam pipes, metal frame and dual sidewheels remain above the waves. By day's end, the death toll stood near 1,021: it was the city's deadliest tragedy until 2001, when 2,753 died in the terrorist attacks on the World Trade Center.

Disasters
IN THE AIR

Help on the way

Survivors of the crash of Uruguayan Air Force Flight 571 hail their rescuers. After their turboprop airplane crashed in the Andes on Oct. 13, 1972, the 16 survivors (out of 45 on the plane) waited for 72 days with no heat and little food until help arrived. They resorted to cannibalism to stay alive

Last Flight of
The *Hindenburg*

May 6, 1937

A titan of the skies bursts into flames, bringing the airship age to an end

TOWARD US, LIKE A GREAT FEATHER ... THE HINDENBURG! *The members of the crew are looking down on the field ahead of them, getting their glimpses of the mooring mast ..."* The voice was that of radio reporter Herbert Morrison, chattering into his microphone at the U.S. Naval Air Station in Lakehurst, N.J. The object of his admiration was the *Hindenburg,* pride of a small fleet of great German airships that was revolutionizing the way people and goods traveled the earth. Once a phenomenon, the craft's transatlantic passage was now routine: the *Hindenburg* had made 10 round trips to the U.S. in 1936. This afternoon's arrival was being covered by radio only because it was the ship's first of 1937. In fact, Morrison's words were not even being broadcast live: he was making a recording to be aired the next day.

It is practically standing still now. The ropes have been dropped and they have been taken hold of by a number of men on the field. It is starting to rain again. The rain has slacked up a little bit. The back motors of the ship are holding it just enough to keep it—

IT'S BURST INTO FLAME!

Get out of the way! Get this—Charley, get out of the way, please! It is bursting into flames. This is terrible! This is one of the worst catastrophes in the world! The flames are 500 ft. into the sky. It is a terrific crash, ladies and gentlemen. It is in smoke and flames now. Oh, the humanity! Those passengers! I can't talk, ladies and gentlemen! Honest, it is a mass of smoking wreckage ... Listen, folks, I am going to have to stop for a minute because I have lost my voice."

A few seconds later, Morrison recovered his voice and continued his recording. But by that time one of the most significant and most completely witnessed and documented disasters in the history of commercial aviation was over: the *Hindenburg* was gone, destroyed in precisely 32 sec. before more than 1,000 appalled onlookers. The ship had lifted off from Frankfurt three days before with 36 passengers, 40 crew members and 21 others approved by the ship's owners aboard. Of the 97 people aboard the aircraft, 35 died in the

Majesty *The* Hindenburg *soars over Manhattan in 1936*

29

Pioneers *Germans were leading the world in airship design when the* Hindenburg *was launched in 1936. Above, the airship touches down in that nation as excited onlookers rush to see it, while a second, unidentified zeppelin passes overhead. In all, the Zeppelin firm designed and flew more than 120 dirigibles from 1900 to 1937, many of them experimental*

calamity, along with one person on the ground. That is not a large death toll when compared with many of the disasters treated in this book. But the demise of the *Hindenburg* claimed more than lives—it also killed a version of the future, putting an end to visions of an era of great airships that could carry people and cargo around the world quickly and safely. Two days after the *Hindenburg* went down in flames, its predecessor, the *Graf Zeppelin,* which had flown some 590 flights around the globe safely since 1928, was pulled out of service. The airship age was over. Today another sort of airship, the blimp, still chugs through the skies, but it survives as a neutered novelty, an advertising medium that provides TV broadcasts with overhead camera views of sporting events.

And what a future was lost when the *Hindenburg* crashed. Pioneered by a wealthy German aristocrat, Count Ferdinand von Zeppelin, the age of the airship began even before the age of the airplane. Zeppelin's first steerable airship, or dirigible, took to the skies in the summer of 1900,

more than three years before the Wright brothers' experimental *Flyer 1* completed its first 12-sec.-long flight. In an age when the novels of H.G. Wells and Jules Verne were dazzling readers with unusual visions of a future powered by new technologies, airships seemed to bring such fictions to buoyant life. Their inventor's name, Zeppelin, became the eponym for the massive but lightweight dirigibles, whose allure outlasted their use by Germany as weapons during World War I.

The 1920s and '30s were the great age of the airship, as zeppelins came into their own as commercial aircraft. In the U.S., the zeppelin *Los Angeles* became a sensation during the excitable Jazz Age, paving the way for the more advanced *Graf Zeppelin* (*Graf* is German for count). Even as U.S. Navy attempts to build rigid airships ended in failure, the *Graf Zeppelin* became the flagship for commercial dirigibles and the model for the later, much more advanced *Hindenburg,* named for Germany's war hero and recent Chancellor, Paul von Hindenburg.

Launched in 1936, the *Hindenburg* dazzled the world

with its size and luxurious amenities. At 803 ft. (245 m) in length and 135 ft. (41 m) in diameter, it was almost as long as three football fields. Its skeleton was formed of 15 main rings made of duralumin, an alloy of aluminum, which separated 16 cotton gas bags filled with lighter-than-air hydrogen gas. At full speed, it traveled at 77 m.p.h. (125 km/h); clipping along with no weather interference, it could cross the Atlantic Ocean in fewer than three days.

Built to serve as a transatlantic passenger vehicle, the *Hindenburg* could carry 40 to 60 crew members and 70 passengers, although 80 people were aboard when the ship completed its hours-long maiden voyage on March 23, 1936. In the months that followed, the new craft traveled across Germany, dazzling enthusiastic crowds wherever it went. Among those who embraced the ship as a potent emblem of German know-how was the nation's Chancellor, Adolf Hitler: on this first triumphant passage, the *Hindenburg* showered Nazi Party propaganda pamphlets upon the cities it flew over.

However, the Nazis were livid that the head of the Zeppelin company, Hugo Eckener, had named the new ship for the man Hitler had replaced as Germany's leader in 1933, Hindenburg. Nazi propaganda chief Joseph Goebbels had proposed a much more suitable name for the craft: the *Adolf Hitler*. Denied naming rights, the party settled for second best. In a tense meeting in 1935, Goeb-

In the control cabin *Ludwig Felber, a "rudderman," is shown at the* Hindenburg's *"header" wheel, directing its forward course, while the second wheel controls its pitch*

Age of the Zeppelin

■ The pioneer of the airship age was Germany's Count Ferdinand von Zeppelin, above. Born in 1838, the nobleman visited the U.S. as an observer during the Civil War, where he was inspired by the lighter-than-air balloons designed by Thaddeus S.C. Lowe, which were used for reconnaissance by Union forces. After serving in the Franco-Prussian War in 1870, the wealthy Zeppelin turned full time to his ideas for a rigid-skeleton, lighter-than-air craft filled with hydrogen and powered and guided by gasoline motors.

Zeppelin's first plans were completed in 1874, but it was not until July 2, 1900, that his first craft, *LZ 1,* lifted off on a wobbly first flight. But within years, Zeppelin's rigid-frame ships were flying regularly and safely, so much so that the count's name became the eponym for steerable lighter-than-air craft, or dirigibles. Germany used zeppelins for reconnaissance in World War I and also to bomb both London and Paris.

Zeppelin died in 1917, as the war was still raging. After Germany surrendered to the Allied powers in 1918, further work on dirigibles was halted under the Treaty of Versailles, as they were seen as weapons of war. But Hugo Eckener, a Zeppelin associate, took over the company and steered it toward commercial use. Under reparations acts, he designed and built airships for use in the U.S. In October, 1924, the first such craft completed a transatlantic flight from Germany to Manhattan, where it was greeted with rapture. Renamed the *Los Angeles,* it became a phenomenon, serving as a successful U.S. passenger ship for eight years before it was retired.

Buoyed by his success, Eckener then developed the *Graf Zeppelin,* the largest and most advanced rigid airship yet made. After its launch in 1928, it became a global sensation, plying the skies safely for nine years and serving as the model for an even more advanced zeppelin, the *Hindenburg.*

bels ordered Eckener to paint Nazi swastikas on all the firm's zeppelins. As it happened, it was just as well for the Nazis that the ship did not bear Hitler's name, for with all its streamlined luxury, the *Hindenburg* was doomed by a design flaw that would cause its famous crash: the hydrogen gas that held it aloft was highly flammable.

When the *Hindenburg* floated into New Jersey on May 6, 1937, it was completing the first half of a planned 18 round trips that year. In command was 45-year-old Captain Max Pruss, a veteran of 170 zeppelin flights across the Atlantic. But the airship was late for its landing. Delayed 12 hours by headwinds in its Atlantic crossing, it reached Labrador at dawn and swam slowly down the coast all day, dipping its nose in courtesy gestures as it passed over Portland, Maine; Boston; and New London, Conn. About 4 p.m. it nuzzled in over Long Island to New York City, while six airplanes buzzed around it. With the sun glinting on its silver-gray sides and the four huge red swastikas on its fins, it circled once over Manhattan, then headed for its berth at Lakehurst. But a sharp thunderstorm came up, and when he reached the naval reservation, Pruss, taking no chances, turned off to sea.

At dusk, while a drizzle fell from a somber sky and a fitful breeze jerked windsocks on the ground, the *Hindenburg* once more poked her nose over Lakehurst and began maneuvering to land. It circled twice, then dropped to 500 ft. (152 m), occasionally spewing the water it used as ballast as it descended.

Below the ship, an excited crowd had gathered to watch the landing. Among those craning their necks to the sky were U.S. airship experts; representatives of the ship's owner, the German Zeppelin Transport Co.; aviation reporters from newspapers, magazines, radio networks and press services; local gawkers; and an elated crowd waving to relatives and friends clustered at the airship's windows, now 300 ft. (91 m) above the ground.

At 7:20 p.m. precisely, two lines fell from the craft's bow. A trained corps of Navy men grabbed one, while a squad of civilians held the other. Gently the two groups began coaxing the big craft to its tall mooring mast, the breeze teasing the tail and making the process more difficult than usual. As Captain Pruss put the two Mercedes-Benz diesel engines in the stern gondolas into reverse to keep from overshooting the mast, witnesses noticed that the port motor was backfiring.

Suddenly a stab of flame gashed the airship's flank near the port stern gondola. Swiftly—so swiftly that to many it seemed instantaneous—the flames engulfed the whole rear half of the ship. With a muffled, booming *whoosh*, a huge belch of white fire and smoke mushroomed sky-

Heyday of the Airship: Inside the *Hindenburg*

■ The *Hindenburg* and the *Titanic*, both destroyed in disasters, illustrate how quickly technology and design were advancing early in the 20th century. Completed in 1912, the doomed ocean liner was ornate, grandiose and heavy; this artifact of the Edwardian age seems a product of the 19th century. Launched 24 years later, the *Hindenburg* was lighter, streamlined, buoyant: a creature of the 20th century.

The *Hindenburg*, of course, plied the skies rather than the seas, and thus was designed to be as lightweight as possible. The passenger quarters, designed by Fritz August Breuhaus, reflected new styles developed at Germany's influential Bauhaus school of design. The chairs in the dining room, shown in the picture at upper right, were made of hollow aluminum tubes and were so light they could be lifted by two fingers, buoyant emblems for the airship itself.

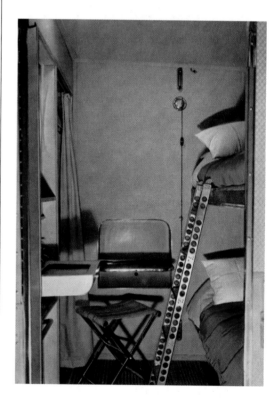

Cramped *The airship's 25 original staterooms were modeled on railroad berths; each had bunk beds and a sink. The ship could carry 70 passengers, who used communal shower rooms. Designed to be light, the ladder was made of perforated aluminum*

Lofty perch *The airship's observation decks featured angled windows that followed the lines of the hull. Flying at low altitudes, generally about 650 ft. (198 m) above the land or water below, zeppelins offered a unique vantage point from which passengers could view the scenes they passed over*

Crew *The* Hindenburg *carried a crew of 50 to 70 on a fully booked flight. The kitchen staff included six male and one female stewards, a chef, four cooks and a messboy.*

The aviation crew included the captain and several pilots, radio operators, riggers, helmsmen and navigators, 17 mechanics, four engineering officers and a ship's doctor

Berths *The passenger quarters of the airship were not located in the gondola that was suspended from its hull; that aerie, whose sides were largely made of glass, was used by the flight crew.*

The passengers were berthed in two levels within the bottom of the hull, which featured observation galleries on both sides of the craft. In addition, the ship held a dining room, a lounge, a study, a bar and even a smoking room

Evidence *These pictures compose a time-lapse sequence of the disaster. At left, the stern was the first section to burst into flames, close to the mooring mast. The bow went down next, as the entire ship collapsed and burned on the ground*

ward. With a *cra-a-a-ack!* the ship buckled. The stern hit the ground first, in a peculiarly gentle crash, amid clouds of dust and smoke. As the still undamaged bow tilted up at 45°, the flame rushed through the middle of the ship and geysered in a long bright plume from the nose. For an instant the *Hindenburg* seemed a rearing reptile darting its tongue in anger. Then it was a gigantic halfback tackled behind the knees and falling forward on its face.

The huge airship began settling slowly to earth with fire still roaring across it at a speed of some 50 yd. (46 m) a second. The flames now reached the passenger quarters nestled in the ship's belly, about one-third of its length back from the bow. Silhouetted by the holocaust, passengers began dropping out of the windows, "like peas from a colander," TIME reported.

As the airship's bow hit the ground, struggling figures emerged from the blazing hulk, stumbled, rose, fell again in fiery suffocation or from broken legs, shock and concussion. The enormous incandescent mass collapsed on the slowest of them, smashing in a blazing blizzard of fabric, crashing girders, melted metal. Still, out of the inferno crept struggling figures, afire from head to foot, some stark naked, their clothes burned away, their skin and flesh in sizzling tatters.

The deep voice of Chief Boatswain's Mate Frederick J. Tobin, in charge of the ground crew, could be heard amid the din: "Navy men, stand fast! We've got to get those people out of there!" Scores of courageous naval aviators and civilians dashed headlong into the conflagration. Though the heat was so intense that thermometers rose in the Navy Aerological School 500 yd. (457 m) away, the rescuers charged into the control cabin and the passenger quarters. An observer was heard to say: "Those boys dived into the flames like dogs after rabbits."

Someone found Ernest Lehmann, a longtime Zeppelin company executive traveling as a passenger, with his clothes frizzled to the skin in back, his hair scorched, his face rutted with third-degree burns, wandering about babbling, "I don't understand it!" over and over. Another led out Captain Pruss, his clothes mostly gone, his lips like two roasted sausages. A naked man staggered out. "I'm all right," he declared, before he fell dead. One rescuer pulled out two dead dogs. Another brought two children, both with broken bones and horrible burns. Seated in a bonfire of debris, one man dazedly slapped at his burning clothes before rescuers doused him with sand and yanked him away.

Ambulances and fire trucks were now clanging in from every direction, even as Lakehurst commander Charles Emery Rosendahl's Navy discipline kept confusion at a minimum. The flames began to subside, but dense black smoke still poured from the twisted heap of red-hot girders and smoldering puddles of fuel oil. Not until the next

morning was the wreckage cool enough to allow the retrieval of all the bodies within, many of them only tentatively identifiable.

The dawn toll of deaths stood at 11 passengers and 21 crew, while 28 passengers and 49 crew miraculously escaped. One member of the ground crew—civilian Allen Hagaman—also died of burns; three more crew members and one more passenger died in the following days. One of the first to pass was Lehmann. Before he died, he declared, "I intended to stay with the ship as long as I could, until we could land her, if possible. But it was impossible. Everything around me was on fire. The windows were open in the central control cabin and I jumped about 100 ft. (30 m). My clothes were all ablaze."

Other survivor stories were equally terse, equally terrible. Passenger Otto Clemens, who jumped safely, told how another passenger, John Pannes, refused to jump until he found his wife; both perished. Mrs. Hermann Doehner related in a husky monotone how she tossed two of her children out of a window, then scrambled out herself with the third. One child died, as did her husband. The others had chances of pulling through. Stewardess Elsa Ernst got away by sliding down a rope. Said she: "I could hear my hair crinkling as it burned." Passenger Herbert O'Laughlin, who ran black-faced into the hangar looking for a telephone to call his mother in Chicago, said, "I was in my cabin … packing … when I felt a slight

First aid *Navy personnel are joined by civilians to aid a badly burned victim of the crash. Naval Air Station Lakehurst in central New Jersey was opened in 1921 to host experiments with lighter-than-air craft, but Navy engineers ended up using German-designed zeppelins*

The remains *An NBC radio broadcast team reports from the site of the crash, above, with the ship's duralumin main rings visible in the background. At right, bodies of the German passengers and crew were returned to their homeland, their coffins draped with swastikas, where they were given a memorial service and hailed as heroes by the Nazi regime*

tremor ... There was very little confusion among the passengers, no screaming, hardly any noise." Captain Pruss said nothing, held incommunicado by doctors who gave him a fifty-fifty chance to live. Though badly burned, the veteran airman did survive.

In Germany it was 2 a.m. when the telephone tinkled by Adolf Hitler's bed at his mountain retreat at Berchtesgaden. After he heard that Germany's greatest transport ship was no more, the Chancellor paced his room the balance of the night, too upset to say anything.

Everywhere in Germany, flags went to half-staff. Nazi-controlled newspapers unanimously exhorted the people to bear up, saying that "young and strong nations" could bear such tragedies. General Hermann Göring, head of the Luftwaffe, declared, "We men of German aviation will still show the world that the idea and the enterprising spirit of Count Ferdinand von Zeppelin are upheld ... We bow to God's will, and at the same time we face the future with an unbending will and passionate hearts."

Why did the great airship explode? As with any disaster, the crash of the *Hindenburg* attracted conspiracy theories

like iron filings to a magnet; they were multiplied by the ship's association with the Nazi Party. In the days after the tragedy, and in the decades that followed, elaborate theories for the cause of crash have been advanced, many involving espionage and Nazi intrigue. But scientists have a good idea of the forces that brought the ship down. The decision to use hydrogen to provide lift, rather than much safer helium, whose world supply was controlled by the U.S., was the root cause of the disaster. The situation was made even more dangerous, some argue, by the company's use of a highly flammable cellulose-based agent to coat the ship's skin in order to add aerodynamic stability. However, this theory has been largely discredited—the photographs of the ship's final moments show that its covering did not catch fire quickly; instead, the flames can be seen emanating from inside the craft.

The cause of the fatal spark that ignited the hydrogen the kept the ship aloft is still unknown: perhaps it came from the afternoon thunderstorm or from the backfiring engine. Yet whatever the genesis of the crash, its outcome is clear: the demise of the *Hindenburg* sent the dirigible on the path of another obsolete beast, the dinosaur. ∎

Future Imperfect

July 25, 2000

A modern icon is mothballed after the supersonic Concorde crashes

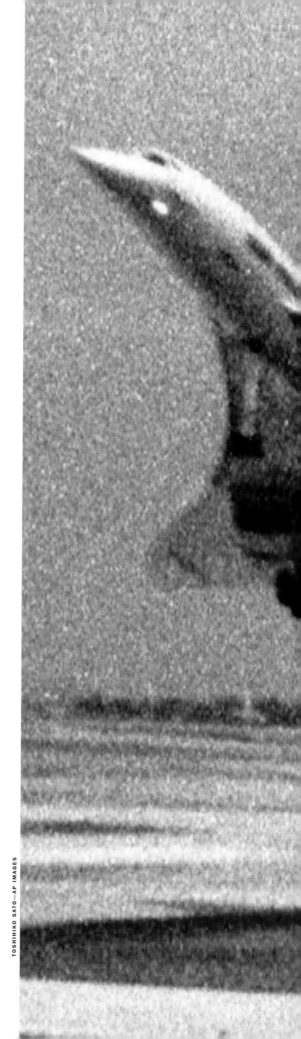

ONCORDE WAS ALWAYS MORE THAN JUST ANOTHER way to travel. From its debut in 1976, the supersonic jetliner, resembling a sleek origami crane, was the embodiment of everything modern. The joint product of Britain and France represented the romance of postwar technology at its most ambitious, like the harnessing of the atom or the Apollo moon landings. And it was fast: the allure of departing London or Paris in the morning and arriving 3.5 hrs. later in New York City never faded. But the trade-offs for the plane's speed were huge: the Concorde had only 100 seats, could carry only a limited amount of luggage, and, as oil prices rose over the decades, became highly expensive to fuel and maintain. Envisioned as a model for future supersonic fleets, it ended up as a rara avis indeed: only 13 Concordes were in regular service when the crash of an Air France jet departing Paris for New York City in 2000 led to the mothballing of the fleet.

The problems began, a later inquiry concluded, when the Concorde's tire hit a strip of titanium dropped from a Continental Airlines DC-10 on the Charles de Gaulle airport runway moments before. The tire shredded, and flying rubber hit the plane's left wing, honeycombed with fuel tanks. Soon a fire was burning in the two left engines, even as it roared down the runway and went airborne, as shown at right. The plane crashed in nearby Gonesse, killing all 109 passengers and crew aboard, as well as four people on the ground. In 2010 a French court ruled both Continental and one of its mechanics were responsible for the crash, finding them guilty on charges of involuntary manslaughter. Both verdicts were under appeal as of early 2012.

Though it took a decade for the judiciary to weigh in, the Concorde had already been convicted in the court of public opinion. British Airways and Air France tried to revive the Concorde after the tragedy, but the supersonic plane had lost its allure. In 2001 a refitted model, sporting tougher tires, made an inaugural flight from London to New York City. It landed safely in the early morning of Sept. 11, 2001, just hours before the 9/11 terrorist attacks. The timing was all too apt: the Concorde was designed for a future that would never be. Two years later, Britain and France declared the great bird would not fly again. ■

Miracle on the Hudson

January 15, 2009

With engine power lost, a gutsy airline captain
ditches his plane and saves 155 lives

A wing and a prayer *Passengers and crew stood on the wings of the plane as it settled into the Hudson River, as a fleet of rescue boats raced to retrieve them*

keep the big jet aloft while gliding over one of the most densely populated cities in the world, with only seconds to concoct and execute a powerless emergency landing.

"It was the worst, sickening, pit-of-your-stomach, falling-through-the-floor feeling I've ever felt in my life," the veteran captain later recalled. With a flight traffic controller, he briefly discussed trying to land at a nearby New Jersey airport, but time—and gravity—forbade that. Sullenberger, then 57, quickly decided that his best course of action was to ditch the plane in the Hudson River. "Brace for impact," he instructed the passengers and cabin crew. The elapsed time from takeoff to loss of thrust in the engines to the landing in the Hudson: 6 minutes.

Said Adam Weiner, an MTV employee who watched the event from an office building: "I was sitting in a conference room on the 39th floor, facing the window. All of a sudden I see a plane gliding into a river. At first I didn't realize what I was seeing. Then spray went up, and you could tell it was a jetliner. Then a couple seconds after, the door blew off and you could see the raft blow up."

In the suspenseful moments that followed, passengers and crew clambered into the raft and onto the wings of the plane, and quick-thinking personnel of boats plying New York Harbor formed an emergency armada of rescue vessels to take them to safety. Meanwhile, within the craft, the steady Sullenberger walked the length of the plane as it slowly settled, ensuring that each of the 154 passengers and other crew aboard had exited safely. Then he turned around and walked the aisle again, just to be sure. The captain was the last person to be plucked from the plane, which was then towed to a pier. New York Governor David Paterson described the safe ditching as "the miracle on the Hudson." America and the world agreed.

What are called "bird and wildlife strikes" have caused hundreds of millions of dollars in damage to U.S. civil and military aviation over the years, as well as loss of life. Not this time: a 1973 graduate of the Air Force Academy, Sullenberger served nearly seven years as an Air Force fighter pilot, then became an airline pilot who took a special interest in safety, helping develop safety protocols for the industry and investigating aviation accidents for the National Transportation Safety Board. The aw-shucks pilot refused to call himself a hero. "It just took some concentration," he said. Maybe so: concentration, plus grace under pressure—plus a whole lot of the right stuff. ■

A FTER LOGGING SOME 19,000 HOURS OF SAFE but anonymous service in the skies, Chesley B. Sullenberger III became a hero in a New York minute. On Jan. 15, 2009, the pilot, known as "Sully," safely guided all 155 passengers and crew aboard US Airways Flight 1549 to an emergency water landing in the city's frigid Hudson River. The Airbus A320's twin engines had both shut down after they sucked in a flock of Canada geese shortly after takeoff from New York City's La Guardia Airport en route to Charlotte, N.C. With both the engines out, Sullenberger found himself fighting to

Crash at an Air Show

September 16, 2011

A vintage fighter plane dives into a crowd, killing 11 people

THE BASIC FORMULA FOR DEADLY DISASTERS hasn't changed much over the years: they occur when unforeseen events challenge underprepared people. But the way we learn about disasters and the way we respond to them have undergone a remarkable change in recent years, as the consumer electronics and Internet revolutions have put the tools of reporting—high-quality still and video cameras—into the hands of millions of us. Today, more than ever before, the film shown on TV news shows and the still pictures that appear in newspapers and magazines are just as likely to have been taken by an amateur as a professional.

The power of this crowdsourced approach to reporting news events was evident in September 2011, when a vintage World War II airplane crashed into a watching crowd at the venerable National Championship Air Races in Reno, Nev. One of the oldest aviation exhibitions in the nation, and the only one that still features racing by vintage planes, the annual event is highly popular, typically drawing 200,000 spectators during its five-day run.

The disaster took place on Sept. 16, as a full house of thousands of aviation buffs crammed the grandstand at the Reno-Stead Airport outside Reno. As the crowd was watching a cluster of seven vintage planes racing in shallow oblong laps that brought them very close to the grandstand, one of the swarm, a Mustang P-51 fighter, which

Out of control *At left, the P-51 Mustang piloted by Jimmy Leeward nose-dives straight into the ground in front of the crowded grandstand. The World War II-era plane left a crater 8 ft. wide by 3 ft. deep (2.4 m by .9 m)*

was flying at about 400 m.p.h., suddenly pitched upward, tipped over on its back and careened straight down, nose-first, descending from a few hundred feet to smash into the runway directly in front of the grandstand, a VIP area where many people were sitting in folding chairs.

"It came down directly at us. As I looked down, I saw the spinner, the wings, the canopy just coming right at us. It hit directly in front of us, probably 50 to 75 feet [away]," Ryan Harris, a spectator in the grandstand, told the Associated Press. "The next thing I saw was a wall of debris going up in the air. That's what I got splashed with."

Within minutes of the crash, even as first responders were treating the injured, spectators who had caught the scene live had uploaded footage of the crash to the Internet. The accident killed 11 people and injured more than 70 others, many of whom were wounded by flying debris.

The pilot of the craft, dead at the scene, was Jimmy Leeward of Ocala, Fla., a 74-year-old veteran barnstormer and movie stunt pilot. In a video posted on YouTube before the Reno show began, Leeward describes a series of modifications he had made to the P-51 fighter, which he christened the *Galloping Ghost,* to improve its speed, including cutting 5 ft. off each wing and shortening the ailerons, the horizontal flaps on the backs of its wings that help balance the craft.

As investigators from the National Transportation Safety Board explored the fatal crash, they viewed many amateur videos of the plane, including footage that appears to show a small aileron, or trim tab, missing on the horizontal tail unit, possibly destabilizing the craft. The NTSB said it will probe the safety of the Reno event in general: 20 pilots have now died at the event over its 48-year run, but no spectators had been injured before 2011.

One witness, commercial pilot Noah Joraanstad, 25, described the diving plane as sounding "like a missile on steroids." But he also pointed out that the crowd did more than photograph the tragedy: many moved quickly to assist the injured. "It was a matter of seconds before spectators started to help and, to me, that is the most amazing part," said Joraanstad, who was burned by flaming fuel and wounded by debris as he fled the impact. "People came into that war zone and started helping." ∎

Deadly Airplane Crashes
The worst of them took place on the ground

TONY COMITI—CORBIS

March 27, 1977

An Inferno in Tenerife Claims 592 Lives

History's greatest air disaster took place on solid ground, when a pair of Boeing 747 jetliners collided on a runway at Los Rodeos Airport on Tenerife, the largest of the Canary Islands, off the coast of Spain. The accident was caused by a bizarre series of events: after a group seeking independence for the Canary Islands set off a bomb at the Gran Canaria airport, many airliners were diverted to the Tenerife airport, packing its runways, even as a dense fog obscured visibility on the ground. The airport lacked ground radar, and control tower operators and pilots were communicating only by radio. Amid the confusion, a KLM flight with 248 aboard tried to take off but instead collided with a Pan Am flight on the runway. In the resulting fires, all those aboard the KLM flight and 344 of 396 people aboard the Pan Am flight perished.

July 17, 1996

The Mysterious Fate of TWA Flight 800

Bound for Paris, TWA Flight 800 took off from JFK International Airport in New York City about 8:18 p.m. on a July evening in 1996, only to explode 12 minutes later and fall into the sea off southern Long Island, killing all 230 people aboard. Witnesses said they had seen an object streaking toward the Boeing 747 before it blew up, and there was much conjecture that the plane had been brought down by a missile, fired either by terrorists or by a U.S. Navy craft in error. Both the National Transportation Safety Board and the FBI conducted extensive inquiries into the crash, but the FBI ruled out the missile theory and the NTSB declared the crash was caused by exploding gas vapors in a fuel tank, most likely ignited by a short circuit. But conspiracy buffs, unsatisfied by both findings, insist that a U.S. government cover-up is preventing the truth from emerging. Above, shards from the craft are being reassembled in 1997.

July 28, 1945

Crash at the Empire State Building

Like the deadly crash of two jetliners in Tenerife in 1977, the 1945 collision of a U.S. Army Air Force bomber with the Empire State Building, then the world's tallest and best-known skyscraper, was the result of dense fog. Transporting military personnel from Bedford, Mass., to La Guardia Airport in Queens, Lieut. Col.. William F. Smith Jr., became disoriented while steering a B-25 Mitchell bomber over Manhattan. The plane smashed into the north side of the building between the 78th and 79th floors.

The 102-story building withstood the collision, a tribute to its builders. And fortunately, July 28 was a Saturday, when many offices were deserted. Even so, 14 people died in the accident: the three aboard the plane and 11 in the building. One of the plane's engines was thrown from the scene and landed on top of a nearby building, badly damaging its penthouse apartment.

Disasters

BY FIRE

Crime scene *The Hayman Fire rages across a hilltop in Teller County, Colo., on June 10, 2002. The largest wildfire in the state's history caused nearly $40 million in damages and burned down 133 homes.*

Sadly, this was not a natural disaster: a U.S. Forest Service employee was convicted of deliberately starting the blaze. Arson is the leading cause of fires in the U.S., accounting for some 317,000 cases each year

CORNER
STATE & MADISON ST
AFTER CHICAGO FIRE

Inferno in The Windy City

October 8-10, 1871

The Great Chicago Fire paves the way for a new, modern metropolis

THE CONFLAGRATION THAT CONSUMED THE city of Chicago in 1871 remains one of greatest American disasters. Among the calamities that have stricken major U.S. cities, only the San Francisco earthquake of 1906, the hurricane that destroyed Galveston in 1900, and the flooding of New Orleans by Hurricane Katrina in 2005 rank with the Great Chicago Fire. And while human errors compounded the impact of those events, they are essentially natural disasters that simply overwhelmed the cities they struck. In contrast, the Chicago fire may have been caused by human action: a bovine suspect, Mrs. Catherine O'Leary's cow, was cleared of all charges long ago.

If we still don't know who started the fire, we do know when and where it began. Around 9 p.m. on the night of Sunday, Oct. 8, 1871, a barn at 137 DeKoven Street that was owned by Patrick and Catherine O'Leary caught fire and burned to the ground. Un-

Devastation *At left, the city center after the fire. Above, an artist portrays citizens fleeing the blaze across the Randolph Street Bridge*

Consumed *This map shows the portion of the city that burned: at the center of the concentric rings is the courthouse, the heart of Chicago in the 19th century. The O'Leary barn on DeKoven Street, where the blaze began, was located in the upper left-hand corner of the burned area shown here. The fire generally moved from south to north, left to right on the map*

der normal conditions, this event might not have led to the devastation of an entire city. But on this fall day, all conditions seemed to conspire to help the flames spread. The city consisted largely of wooden structures, excellent kindling at any time, but especially so that autumn, when a 14-week drought had dried out the lumber in the city's houses. Moreover, the 216 firefighters charged with responding to metropolitan blazes were exhausted from fighting a different, major fire only the day before; their responses were sluggish and indecisive, multiplying the effects of the tragedy. As 19th century historian A.T. Andreas declared, in a sentence worthy of Gibbon, "Nature had withheld her accustomed measure of prevention, and man had added to the peril by recklessness."

A barn had burned, but it was the events that followed that mattered: the fire was allowed to spread, and soon it was out of control. Through a series of missteps that amounted to a tragedy of errors, firefighters misunderstood the alarm bells that began ringing in firehouses after 9 p.m., and some of them were actually dispatched

in the wrong direction. As the fire grew, it became a small but deadly weather system of its own. The O'Leary barn was in the city's Near West Side, just north of the South Fork of the Chicago River. A strong breeze blowing from the southwest combined with superheated winds from the flames to create a powerful draft that hurled flaming brands into the air, driving the fire northeast. The fire was moving fast: first it jumped across the South Fork of the Chicago River, then it hopped the main branch of the river, which divides downtown Chicago into the sprawling South Side and the more prosperous North Side.

Now a mighty force of nature, the fire's flames feasted on the wooden houses, sidewalks, piers, boats and, yes, massive lumberyards of this city largely composed of timber. Citizens roused from slumber clogged the streets and the river bridges, with many on the North Side seeking refuge in Lincoln Park or along the shores of Lake Michigan. After the disaster, tales of drunkenness and looting spread; no doubt there was some of both, but the overall reaction seems to have been one of mass panic and flight.

Firefighters had been unable to contain the fire at any

point, but when the municipal Pumping Station on the North Side went up in flames around 3:30 a.m., all hopes of stopping the conflagration evaporated. Flight was the only option that remained.

On the South Side, where the blaze had begun, flames devoured some of the city's best-known structures, including the Palmer House Hotel and the offices of the Chicago *Tribune*. The damage on the North Side was much more severe and far more extensive, although a lovely new stone water tower on Michigan Avenue managed to survive the inferno. Over the decades, it has become an unofficial emblem of the great disaster.

The fire raged around the clock on Monday and into Tuesday before it began to die down, as a light drizzle began to quench the flames. When the dazed citizens took stock of their ruined city, the extent of the tragedy began to sink in. Chicago had lost some 18,000 buildings (13,000 of which were on the North Side). Some 100,000 citizens had been left homeless, and the loss in property value was estimated at $200 million, about one-third of the city's entire valuation. Some 4 sq. mi. of the city was utterly devastated. The good news: the loss of life was not overwhelming. While it's impossible to get a firm death count, it is believed that some 300 people died.

So ... whodunit? Who started the Great Chicago Fire? The story that Mrs. O'Leary's cow kicked over a lantern, starting the blaze, makes for a fine tale. But it is only a tale, as the newspaperman who invented it, Michael Ahern, eventually revealed. More convincing are the accusations against the O'Learys' neighbor, Daniel ("Peg Leg") Sullivan, the first to report the blaze. Modern students of the calamity suspect Sullivan may have started the fire while stealing milk from the O'Leary barn. Another strong suspect is Louis Cohn, only 18 in 1871. In his 1944 will, the businessman claimed he had been gambling with some other youngsters in the O'Leary barn when Patrick O'Leary came out to evict them; in their haste, one of them kicked over a lantern, igniting the hay in the barn. But Cohn provided little proof to support his story.

We may never know the origin of the Great Chicago Fire. But we do know its outcome: harnessing the propulsive, can-do spirit for which Chicago is known, its citizens rebuilt their city of wood as a city of steel, brick and glass. Two decades of engineering breakthroughs followed the fire: hydraulic elevators, fireproof hollow tile, new foundation planning and steel-skeleton building construction. The dazzling result is the foremost U.S. contribution to architecture, the skyscraper. The ill winds of the Great Chicago Fire cleared the ground for the creation of the modern template for metropolises. ∎

TOP: CHICAGO HISTORY MUSEUM (2); BOTTOM: COPELIN & HINE—CHICAGO HISTORY MUSEUM

Aftermath *After the fire, magazines and books were filled with anecdotes from the disaster. At top, a family perishes together on a blazing rooftop. Above, a wedding ceremony is conducted amid the ruins, with a soapbox serving as an impromptu altar. Below, customers patronize the first general store to open after the fire; the al fresco market sold cigars, grapes and apples, promising "old prices"*

Out of control *The fire raged through the top three floors of the Asch Building, above. At right, a policeman watches as people jump from the building, with several dead bodies around him*

Tragedy in a Sweatshop

March 25, 1911

A fire kills 146 workers, most of them female, and results in the passage of new laws to protect laborers

THE RAPID GROWTH OF THE GARMENT INDUSTRY IN NEW YORK CITY AT THE turn of the 20th century brought a large number of young, unmarried women into the workplace. Often forced to work in sweatshops, they were easily exploited by their employers but drew upon a spirit of independence to begin organizing trade unions and pro-labor newspapers. In 1909 a general strike of garment-industry workers was called, and 20,000 to 30,000 laborers, the majority of them women, joined the protest. One of the targets of their anger was the city's largest maker of women's blouses, the Triangle Shirtwaist company, located on the top floors of the 10-story Asch Building near Washington Square Park in Greenwich Village. The firm's owners, Max Blanck and Isaac Harris, were known for maintaining tight discipline and for disregarding fire and safety measures.

Only two years later, on a bright spring Saturday, March 25, 1911, a fire broke out at closing time inside the Triangle workspace. Fueled by hundreds of pounds of highly flammable cotton and tissue scraps, the blaze spread quickly through the building's top three floors. Hundreds of onlookers converged as horse-drawn fire engines thundered from every direction. Yet, to their immense frus-

Incinerated *This photograph shows the 10th floor of the Asch Building, with its interior completely gutted and only the floors and walls standing. Workers on the eighth and 10th floors generally escaped the blaze, but those on the ninth floor were trapped*

tration, the firefighters soon found that their equipment was not powerful enough to fight the fire: built for an earlier era, their ladders were unable to reach higher than the seventh floor. In the building, workers on the eighth and 10th floors were able to escape unharmed, but those on the ninth floor were not so lucky. Trapped by a locked door, they began to leap to their deaths.

A United Press reporter who witnessed the scene wrote that he learned "a new sound—a more horrible sound than description can picture. It was the thud of a speeding, living body on a stone sidewalk." About 50 of the factory's young women workers, some of them flaming human torches, crashed to the sidewalk; none of them survived. Over 100 more died in the building. According to the UP reporter, water pumped into the building by the firemen ran red in the gutter. By the time the last victim succumbed to her injuries, the toll was 146 dead: 129 of them women, dozens of them teenagers.

An article in the New York *World* newspaper the next day listed close to half a dozen avoidable circumstances that contributed to the high death toll: "A single fire escape, a single stairway, one working elevator ... life nets

either torn from grasp of rescuers or burst by force of numbers ... fireproof doors were locked." The cause of the fire was never determined, although many observers have speculated that it was caused by a cigarette or match.

It's often said that the tragedy was so gruesome that New Yorkers could not possibly look away and forget. But that underestimates the vast and awful store of history that humans have gladly forgotten. The real reason we remember the Triangle fire is its legacy, not its toll. The full story of this disaster is not simply a frightening tale of greedy, reckless owners and exploited workers who died as a result of their employers' negligence. As TIME editor-at-large David Von Drehle, author of *Triangle: The Fire That Changed America,* argues, it remains a compelling study of political power, as relevant today as it was in the angry aftermath of that inferno.

At the dawn of the 20th century, New York City had been run for more than a generation by the corrupt Democratic political machine known as Tammany Hall. Boss Charles F. Murphy ruled the city from his private room at Delmonico's restaurant, quietly tending the gears that turned the votes of poor immigrants into power and profit for Tammany. But new waves of immigrants were filling the grim tenements of Manhattan, and many of them weren't content to do the Tammany ward heelers' bidding. Especially among the East European Jews who fled the oppression of the dying Russian Empire, a spirit of independence led the new arrivals to organize their own institutions to advance their views and interests.

They first made their numbers known with their strike for better wages and union recognition in the autumn of 1909. The following year, an even larger strike by the men of the cloakmakers' union created a model for modern industrial relations. Now, on April 5, two weeks after the fire, more than 100,000 people marched in a memorial parade up Fifth Avenue, as 400,000 spectators watched.

Murphy had always taken the side of management— but his genius was the ability to count votes. He saw that the Triangle fire was a chance to win over the voters of this new generation. Acting quickly, he created a powerful Factory Investigating Commission, led by two bright young Tammany lawmakers, Robert F. Wagner and Alfred E. Smith. Over the next three years, the commission proposed and passed in New York State the most pro-

gressive agenda of workplace reforms the U.S. had ever seen. From 1912 through 1914, 13 of 17 commission bills submitted became law. This new and much stricter code of state factory safety and health laws included measures requiring better fire safety efforts; more adequate factory ventilation; improved sanitation; safe operation of elevators; and special measures for foundries, bakeries, stores and other establishments. The new laws were widely copied in other states and by the Federal Government.

Sadly, factory owners Blanck and Harris did not pay a price for the deaths caused by their negligent and inhumane policies. Though the two men were indicted on charges of manslaughter, they were later acquitted and actually profited from insurance claims.

At a ceremony on March 25, 2011, the centennial of the calamity, the names of all the victims of the Triangle fire were read aloud for the first time, thanks to genealogist Michael Hirsch, who unearthed the identities of six previously unidentified victims of the fire. After 100 years, their legacy of safer workplaces, free of harassment and exploitation, is more real for us than they might have imagined on that doomed Saturday in March 1911. ∎

Grim duty *Families of the deceased visit the New York City morgue to identify the dead. Six victims' names were revealed in 2011*

Horror in Halifax

December 6, 1917

A munitions ship blows up, leveling Nova Scotia's capital city

PERCHED MAJESTICALLY around one of the world's largest natural harbors, Halifax, Nova Scotia's capital, is one of Canada's most charming cities. Modern-day visitors who stroll through its Public Gardens may feel as if they have traveled in time as well as space, back to the graceful, civilized days of the Edwardian era. Yet it was here that one of the greatest man-made explosions in history took place, after a Norwegian cargo ship collided with a French munitions ship during World War I.

The Halifax Explosion, the largest in human history before the atomic age, became the standard by which such blasts are measured. "When the munitions ship *Mont-Blanc* exploded in the harbor of Halifax, N.S., on Dec. 6, 1917, the shock was felt more than 150 miles away," TIME declared in August 1945. "The explosion killed more than 1,100, laid waste two square miles of the city ... The single atomic bomb which fell on Hiroshima in Japan this week exploded with approximately seven times the force of that tremendous charge."

If the blast was historic, its origins were mundane: Halifax Harbor, a major port for ships making the transatlantic crossing from Europe, was bustling throughout World War I, as Canadian troops shipped out for the front and wounded veterans returned home. Large convoys of ships bound across the Atlantic that sought safety in numbers from German U-boat attacks gathered in the Bedford Basin section of the port, where they were protected the old-fashioned way: each night, heavy iron nets were fixed in place to forbid entry to the enemy submarines.

But iron nets can't prevent human error, and through a

series of ill-judged maneuvers, the Norwegian steamer S.S. *Imo,* chartered by a Belgian relief organization and bound for New York City to take on a load of supplies, collided with a French cargo ship, S.S. *Mont-Blanc. A* floating munitions dump, that ship carried 2,300 tons of wet and dry nitrogen-based picric acid, 200 tons of TNT and 35 tons of benzoyl, a highly explosive oil product, stored in the open on its decks.

The two vessels crashed together around 8:45 a.m., starting a fire on the *Mont-Blanc*; its crew, fearing a blast, hastily abandoned ship. The French ship exploded 19 minutes later, sending a shock wave across the city that not only destroyed the ship, but also hurled a portion of its anchor 2.5 miles (4 km) away, leveled a majority of the buildings within a 16-mile (26 km) radius, killed some 1,950 people and injured 9,000 more. The blast even blew away the water in the bay, exposing the seabed; the resulting vacuum created a roaring tsunami that rose in places to 59 ft. (18 m) and claimed many victims.

As the city lay devastated, nature added a final burden to its misery: one of the largest blizzards in Halifax's history set in that night, hampering rescue and relief efforts even as some 25,000 homeless people struggled to survive. In the grim months that followed, the city battled to bury the dead and feed and shelter the living. A massive relief campaign was mounted, with another seaport city, Boston, leading it. Today, a restored and reshaped Halifax is thriving—and each year it recalls its tragedy in greenery, as a Christmas tree shipped from Nova Scotia graces Boston Common in remembrance of the U.S. city's charity. ∎

Shock wave *The walls of many buildings buckled from the blast, above. At left, the smoke from the explosion fills the sky*

Leveled *A crowd seeks survivors, a process that was later set back when a blizzard dropped 16 in. (40 cm) of snow on the city*

57

Stampede in a Nightclub

November 28, 1942

A fire at Boston's largest dance hall kills 492 people

BOSTON WAS BUZZING ON THE NIGHT OF Nov. 28, 1942: it was Thanksgiving weekend, and, in a long-awaited football game between local teams, unheralded Holy Cross had upset No. 1–ranked Boston College that afternoon, 55-12. Crowds of sports fans joined soldiers and sailors in uniform at the city's hottest club, Cocoanut Grove, that Saturday night. The tropical-themed nightclub sprawled over a one-and-a-half-story area whose focal point was a big dance floor upstairs that gave way to a maze of smaller private dining rooms. The club was a favorite with Boston's organized-crime crowd: former owner Charles ("Boston Charlie") Solomon had been gunned down at a rival establishment in 1933, and current boss Barney Welansky was a tough operator who liked to keep firm tabs on his customers—so firm that he kept most of the club's exits, including those provided for emergencies, locked up to keep customers from departing without paying their bill.

Fire codes called for no more than 600 patrons to occupy the Cocoanut Grove, but for Welansky, laws were for flouting: authorities later estimated that more than 1,000 people were packed into the big club when busboy Stanley Tomaszewski, only 16, went to screw a new light bulb into a socket in the downstairs Melody Lounge around 10:15 p.m. When he lit a match to get his bearings, Tomaszewski apparently ignited one of the fake palm trees in the lounge (the fire's cause is still officially undetermined). Soon, as TIME told the story, "the fire quickly ate away the palm tree, raced along silk draperies, was sucked upstairs through the stairway, leaped along ceiling and

Before and after *At left, Cocoanut Grove emcee Mickey Alpert, in tuxedo, greets servicemen performing in Irving Berlin's show* This Is the Army *30 minutes before the blaze erupted; all survived. At center, firefighters clean up the ruins of the club's bar. On right, a bystander carries a woman who survived the flames away from the club*

wall. The silk hangings, turned to balloons of flame, fell on table and floor. Men and women fought their way toward the revolving door [at the front of the club]; the push of bodies jammed it. Near by was another door; it was locked tight. There were other exits, but few Cocoanut Grove patrons knew about them. The lights went out. There was nothing to see now except flame, smoke and weird moving torches that were men and women with clothing and hair afire."

Caught up in the horrifying stampede, patrons struggled to find exits from the club, now a vaulted oven. Firefighters had to dismantle the main revolving door to enter the building, clearing their way through a pile of bodies six deep. Two escape doors elsewhere in the club opened inward and were quickly clogged with bodies; authorities later estimated that if the doors had opened outward, as many as 300 of those who died may have survived.

Yet there were heroes amid the horror. Coast Guardsman Clifford Johnson, 21, escaped the blaze only to venture back into the inferno four times, looking for his date. He had no way of knowing that she had escaped and was looking for him in the streets. Johnson was burned over 55% of his body but made a full recovery, a medical feat so remarkable that TIME devoted a story to it in 1943.

The impact of the disaster rivaled that of the fire at the Triangle Shirtwaist Factory in Manhattan in 1911: the death toll was so high, and the particulars of the tragedy so revolting, that legislators could not ignore them. In the next few years, laws were passed in Massachusetts and many other states that banned flammable decorations in clubs, mandated the presence of outward-opening doors on either side of revolving doors and forbade the closure of emergency exits for any reason.

Welansky, whose connections with authorities had helped him violate existing fire laws, was convicted on 19 counts of manslaughter. He served more than three years in prison, then was freed in the weeks before he died from cancer. Johnson, the heroic survivor, met a less just fate: as TIME reported in 1956, "Last week ... Johnson was driving a truck near Jefferson City, Mo. He missed a turn, and his truck crashed into a ditch, caught fire. Clifford Johnson was burned to death." ■

Tragedy Under The Big Top

July 6, 1944

A circus fire kills 169 people and takes a great show off the road

T HE CIRCUS EXISTS IN AN ALTERNATE WORLD, where alliteration accumulates and life passes in capital letters. A 1932 TIME cover story on the Ringling Bros. and Barnum & Bailey Circus quoted a ringmaster who described a simple parade of elephants thusly: "AFTER THEIR AMAZING ACTS, THESE HUGE BEASTS, AUGMENTED BY YET OTHERS, WILL BE MASSED IN FORMIDABLE FORMATION, PRESENTING THE MOST IMPOSING ELEPHANTINE COLUMN OF ALL TIME."

And so on. Yet no Barnumesque ballyhoo was needed to underscore one of the Ringling troupe's grandest boasts: it was the largest traveling entertainment spectacle ever mounted. For decades, the day the circus came to town amounted to a local holiday wherever its train wheezed to a stop. After a parade through the streets—mobile advertising—an imposing elephantine col-

umn was harnessed to long timber poles and pulled them upright to support the famous Big Top, a canvas tent vast enough to cover the show's three rings and shelter more than 10,000 spectators from the elements.

The circus was an integral element of American life. Yet unlike the vaudeville circuit or even the racist minstrel shows of the 19th century, the circus survived nearly unchanged until deep into the 20th century, still bearing the name

Exodus *Many spectators were able to escape the blazing Big Top—but not all survived*

61

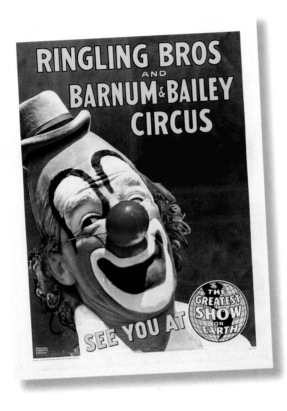

of the celebrated master of 19th century showmanship, Phineas T. Barnum.

When the circus came to town, it created a second town. The Ringling train that pulled into Hartford, Conn. early in July 1944, carried some 1,000 animals, scores of performers and musicians and hundreds of support staff: cooks and cleaners, seamstresses and mechanics, roustabouts and wranglers. This was truly THE GREATEST SHOW ON EARTH, and a crowd of some 8,000 people packed the Big Top for the matinee performance on July 6. It was a workday, and most of the spectators were women and children. As the show's second feature performers, Alfred Court's lions, tigers and leopards, were leaving the main ring and the Flying Wallenda aerialists were preparing to begin their act, some spectators noticed a tiny lick of flame ascending the Big Top canvas.

Three ushers ran to quench the growing flames with buckets of water but were driven back by the heat, as the fire spread across the canvas with lightning speed. "It was hardly bigger than a cigarette burn, then it burst through, suddenly in a big common flame and went flying around the place," according to local policeman James F. Healy. As TIME reported: "The bleachers suddenly rumbled under thousands of feet; folding chairs clattered and banged. The crowd struggled to reach the ground, flowed wildly toward the exits, clotted into groups which pushed and elbowed with silent, furious concentration in the furnace-

like heat. Men and women in the high bleacher seats began dropping children to the ground, then jumped themselves. Then great blazing patches of canvas fell. Women screamed as their hair and dresses caught fire. Then a tent pole toppled soundlessly, trailed by burning canvas. People were still struggling down from their seats. Three minutes had passed."

Bandmaster Merle Evans ordered the ensemble to play *The Stars and Stripes Forever,* the troupe's "disaster march"—the signal to every carny on the lot that an emergency was at hand. And the troupers responded, but as one roustabout later recalled, "It was like you had opened Hell's doors, and you had all you could do to get your hands over your face and run the other way."

The band kept playing as the majority of the spectators fled safely. But not all succeeded: when the blaze was finally extinguished, and the death toll was taken, 169 had died—perhaps half of them children. Later inquiries focused on a number of reasons why the fire spread so quickly, with investigators blaming the troupe for using a paraffin-based substance, mixed with gasoline, to waterproof the canvas on the Big Top. Local fire and police authorities were also blamed for not following safety codes: the tent was not inspected by local firefighters before it was erected, and other safety protocols were not enforced.

Six circus employees were soon found guilty of criminal negligence; five of them served time in prison but were later paroled. The source of the fire was not established. Some thought a discarded cigarette might have sparked it, while others suspected an electrical short circuit. It was not until 1950 that a more likely suspect emerged. In an Ohio courtroom, Robert D. Segee, then 21, confessed to having committed arson in Hartford while working as a roustabout. But Segee had a history of mental illness; found guilty of other arson charges, he was sentenced to 40 years in prison. He may have started the Hartford fire, or he may have been grandstanding. The cause of the blaze remains officially unknown.

Yet whatever agency started the fire, it ended up stopping the great traveling days of the circus. The Ringling troupe toured America by train for a few more years, but in 1956 the Big Top was formally retired. The circus endures, but the pomp and pageantry of its peripatetic passages are now part and parcel of the past. ■

Tears of a clown *Emmett Kelly, the Ringling troupe's beloved tramp clown, was one of the company's biggest draws. A photographer caught him carrying water to fight the fire, and the picture ran in newspapers across the country, leading Americans to christen the tragedy "the day the clowns cried"*

Deadly U.S. Fires

Conflagrations in crowded places breed panic—and death

LEFT, TOP: AP IMAGES; BOTTOM: RICHARD DIAZ—U.S. AIR FORCE—AP IMAGES. RIGHT, TOP: C.J. GUNTHER—REUTERS—CORBIS; INSET: JOE GIRON—CORBIS. BOTTOM: BETTMANN CORBIS

November 21, 1980

The MGM Grand Fire

"Tired and dazed, the guests waited to be escorted to their smoke-blackened rooms to retrieve belongings," TIME reported after a fire at the MGM Hotel on the Las Vegas Strip killed 85 people and injured more than 700 in 1980. "Passing motorists slowed on Flamingo Road to gawk and snap pictures. Inside, firemen sloshed through the gutted casino, trying to puzzle out how the blaze began."

The culprit, inquiries found, was a short circuit in an electrical wire in the hotel delicatessen. Most of the dead were guests trapped on the upper floors, who perished of smoke inhalation. It was the second-deadliest hotel fire in U.S. history, after Atlanta's 1946 Winecoff Hotel blaze, which killed 119 people.

February 20, 2003

The Station Nightclub Fire

When popular '80s rock group Great White took the stage of the Station, a rock club in West Warwick, R.I., early in 2003, "gerbs"—sparking fireworks fountains—shot up from the stage. Within seconds, flames crawled up the sound-proof foam panels behind the band and spread to the 9-ft. (2.7 m) -high ceiling. As heat and black smoke billowed through the packed club, patrons stampeded for the exits. Within minutes, 100 people had died and 230 were injured. Great White guitarist Ty Longley, 31, at left in the inset photo, was among the dead. The band's manager accepted a plea bargain on charges of involuntary manslaughter and served less than 2 years in prison; the club's owners pleaded "no contest" to similar charges; one served more than 2 years in prison, and the other was given a suspended sentence.

December 30, 1903

Chicago's Iroquois Theater Fire

The final death toll remains unknown for the deadliest theater fire in U.S. history, but most experts believe slightly more than 600 people out of a crowd of some 2,000 died when the building caught fire at year's end in 1903. The victims were mainly women and children. The Iroquois Theater had been promoted as "absolutely fireproof"—but its owners opened it prematurely late in 1903 to meet holiday demand, though it did not yet meet safety regulations.

The fire began when an arc light over the stage shorted out, igniting a curtain. Actor Eddie Foy came onstage and begged the crowd to maintain order, but panic erupted when many exit doors would not open. Amid the stampede, many died of smoke inhalation. The tragedy led to the adoption and enforcement of a number of new fire-safety measures in theaters, including use of the "panic bar," which helps people open doors outward in the event of an emergency.

Disasters
OF THE ENVIRONMENT

Dirty work *A volunteer collects solidified oil sludge on the coast of Ons Island off north-west Spain. On Nov. 13, 2002, a tank burst on the oil tanker* Prestige *during a storm; six days later the ship split in two and sank, releasing more than 60,000 tons of oil that polluted the coastlines of Spain and Portugal. The good news: residents along the coast organized a clean-up campaign that largely mitigated the damage from the spill*

Of Hurricanes And Humans

August 29, 2005

Bad weather and bad planning devastate New Orleans

AMERICANS WATCHED IN HORROR IN 2005 as Hurricane Katrina manhandled New Orleans, one of the nation's most historic and culturally influential cities. As levees collapsed and storm surges pushed water into the low-lying city, civil order broke down and government officials at all levels—civic, state and federal—proved unable to mount a response equal to the magnitude of the crisis.

In the weeks after the calamity, the story line of Katrina seemed simple enough: a huge natural disaster had overwhelmed the Crescent City. Yet as TIME correspondent Michael Grunwald has argued in a series of articles for the magazine, the story is far more complex. "The most important thing to remember about the drowning of New Orleans," Grunwald wrote in 2007, "is that it wasn't a natural disaster. It was a man-made disaster, created by lousy engineering, misplaced priorities and pork-barrel politics."

Katrina was not the Category 5 killer—the Big One—that the Big Easy had always feared; it was a Category 3 storm that missed New Orleans, where it was at worst a weak Category 2. The city's defenses should have withstood its surges, and if they had, Americans would never have seen the squalor in the Superdome, the desperation on the rooftops, the shocking tableau of the Mardi Gras city underwater for weeks. The Federal Emergency Management Agency (FEMA) became the scapegoat, but the real culprit was the U.S. Army Corps of Engineers, which bungled the building of the levees that formed the city's man-made defenses

Overwhelmed *Water flows across a damaged levee along the Inner Harbor Navigation Canal in New Orleans, 80% of which flooded after Hurricane Katrina breached many of the city's levees*

Where to turn? *As New Orleans flooded, electrical power was lost in much of the city, and officials, particularly at the Federal Emergency Management Agency, seemed unprepared to deal with the disaster. Above, citizens seek higher ground and safety*

and ravaged the wetlands that once formed its natural defenses. "Americans were outraged by the government's response, but they still haven't come to grips with the government's responsibility for the catastrophe," Grunwald argued.

Indeed, as Katrina hit New Orleans, there were 28 reported levee failures on Aug. 29 and more than 50 more breaches were reported in the ensuing days. These failures, in addition to multiple breaches of two major man-made waterways, the Mississippi River–Gulf Outlet canal (MRGO) and the Industrial Canal, allowed floodwaters, driven by storm surges, to inundate entire sections of the city, much of which lies below sea level.

New Orleans wasn't always a city in a bowl, however. The French founded it in 1718 on high ground along the Mississippi, a "natural levee" of sediment deposited by the river. That's why tourists in the French Quarter stayed dry during Katrina. And that's how all of south Louisiana was built—by the Mississippi River mutinying its banks and rambling around its floodplain like an unruly teenager, dropping mud around its delta and creating roughly 4.5 million acres of wetlands between New Orleans and the Gulf. So while the French built an earthen levee one

mile long and 3 ft. high (1.6 km long, 1 m high) to block the river's annual tantrums, they didn't bother trying to block the occasional hurricanes that swept up the Gulf. "They didn't need hurricane levees," Kerry St. Pe, a marine biologist whose ancestors arrived in 1760, told Grunwald. "They had wetlands to protect them." New Orleans wasn't on the coast, and hurricanes wilt over land.

Now the Gulf has advanced some 20 miles (32 km) inland, thanks in large part to the Army Corps. The Corps started as a Revolutionary War regiment, fortifying Bunker Hill, but it evolved into an all-purpose engineering unit, eventually overseeing local flood control on the Mississippi. The Corps ordered communities to imprison the river in a narrow channel with a strict "levees only" policy, rejecting calls to give the river room to spread out. So levees rose, and the Corps repeatedly declared the river floodproof. But the constrained river also rose, and its jailbreaks repeatedly proved the Corps wrong. In the epic flood of 1927, crevasses in the levees shredded the entire Mississippi valley and nearly destroyed New Orleans.

Congress soon rewarded this failure by allowing the Corps to seize control of the entire river and its tributaries, an unprecedented Big Government project that foreshadowed the New Deal and established the Corps as the U.S.'s manipulator of water and manhandler of nature. It built dams, floodways, revetments and pumped-up levees throughout the Mississippi basin, caging the beast in its channel, safeguarding riverfront cities, creating a reliable web of liquid highways. But by walling off the river, trapping its sediments behind giant dams and armoring its erosive banks with concrete, the Corps choked off the land-building process. The straitjacketed river now carries less than half its original sediment load down to Louisiana. So there's little new land-building material to offset the natural erosion of the coast, much less the unnatural rising of the sea fueled by global warming. During the past century, 2,300 sq. mi. (5,960 sq km) of Louisiana's coastal marshes, barrier islands and cypress swamps have eroded into the Gulf of Mexico.

The result is that New Orleans is sinking, and about 30% of the coast's wetlands have slipped into the Gulf, jutting Louisiana's chin even further into the path of Mother Nature's fist, endangering the U.S.'s largest offshore oil and gas fields, a lucrative seafood industry, a busy network of ports and about 2 million people. Oil and gas canals have accelerated the land losses. But so have Corps navigation canals, especially the notorious MRGO, a shipping shortcut from the Gulf coast to the Port of New Orleans that was a larger dirt-moving project than the Panama Canal when it opened in 1965.

The canal never carried many ships, but it has carried plenty of saltwater into freshwater marshes and cypress forests, killing nearly 100 sq. mi. (259 sq km) of wetlands. Shortly before Katrina, Louisiana State University hydraulic engineer Hassan Mashriqui called the MRGO a "critical and fundamental flaw" in New Orleans' defenses; after Katrina, his modeling found that the outlet boosted Katrina's surge 2 ft. (0.6 m) and increased its velocity 10-fold, overwhelming St. Bernard Parish and the Lower Ninth Ward. "This was a disaster created by the Corps," Mashriqui says. Even the Corps eventually agreed; it closed the MRGO canal for good in 2009.

The Crescent City still might have fended off Katrina if its levees hadn't played matador defense. After Hurricane Betsy pummeled the city in 1965, Congress assigned the Corps to protect the city from a 100-year storm. The agency's first mistake, acting against the counsel of the National Weather Service, was calculating that 100-year event as a modest Category 3 hurricane, even though Betsy had been a 4. The Corps then made such egregious engineering errors that it wasn't even ready for a smaller storm. For example, its levees sagged as much as 5 ft. (1.5 m) lower than their design because the Corps miscalculated sea level and then failed to adjust for subsidence. Some were built in soils with the stability of oatmeal.

Five years after Katrina flooded New Orleans, a new peril threatened the Gulf Coast, in a disaster that was entirely the work of man: the 2010 BP Deepwater Horizon oil spill. The images of oiled pelicans called attention to the ailing coast in a way that Katrina never did, inspiring warnings that the spill could further degrade eroding marshes and push a stressed ecosystem toward its tipping point. These turned out to be false alarms: coastal evaluation teams have discovered less than 1,000 acres of oiled wetlands from the BP spill, while Katrina and the subsequent Hurricane Rita wiped out 130,000 acres. But as Grunwald noted, "The coast is still sliding into the Gulf. And the Big One is still on the way." ■

Hauled to safety *A U.S. Coast Guard helicopter plucks a New Orleans resident from a flooded neighborhood. The Coast Guard was one federal agency that was widely praised for mounting an effective response to the city's plight*

The Johnstown Flood

May 31, 1889

A flimsy dam collapses, and a Pennsylvania town is destroyed

THE JOHNSTOWN FLOOD HAS NEVER LOST its hold on the American imagination. Here is the stuff of nightmares: a small town, clinging to the sides of a narrow gorge in the mountains, is devastated as a towering wall of floodwaters roars through the ravine, sweeping all before it. If this were only the story of a flood, it would be terrifying. But it is also a story of a chain of human errors in judgment, errors that condemned to death more than 2,200 people in this hamlet, some 66 miles (106 km) outside Pittsburgh.

The town's fate was largely decided by its location: nestled deep in the hills of southwestern Pennsylvania, it was prone to flooding whenever heavy rains swelled Stony Creek and the Little Conemaugh River, which con-

verge in the center of the town at a place called the Point.

The town numbered some 30,000 residents in 1889. To its east, high in the hills, was Lake Conemaugh, an artificial reservoir created by the South Fork Dam, which was completed in 1853 by the State of Pennsylvania as part of a canal system. When railroads made canals obsolete, the dam and reservoir were sold to a railroad line which in turn sold it to private interests. Eventually, the site was purchased by a group of wealthy Pennsylvanians, including steel magnates Henry Clay Frick and Andrew Carnegie, who converted it into the South Fork Fishing and Hunting Club, a private recreational compound.

The dam, which stood 72 ft. (22 m) high, had been allowed to deteriorate since the railroad bought it. It fre-

Fire and water *This contemporary illustration captures one of the most unusual incidents of the disaster. When floodwaters bearing trees and lumber piled up against a stone railroad bridge, the wood ignited, burning to death some 80 people. The fire blazed for three days before it was extinguished. At left, survivors gather amid the ruins of the town after the tragedy*

quently sprang leaks, and one short-term owner had removed and sold for scrap three metal pipes that helped control run-off. Further renovations under the club's ownership lowered the height of the dam and eliminated drainage, making it even more vulnerable to heavy rains.

Those rains, a deluge of them, came at the end of May 1889, when some 6 to 10 in. (152 to 254 mm) of water fell in 24 hours, swelling Lake Conemaugh and threatening the dam. Despite frantic exertions to buttress the structure, it collapsed around 3:10 p.m., sending 20 million tons of water cascading downhill toward Johnstown. Along the way, the torrent collected trees, animals, boulders, shards from shattered houses, rolls of barbed wire from an ironworks it crushed—whatever was in its path. One eyewitness described the floodwaters as resembling "a huge hill, turning over and over."

The flood stopped briefly when it butted up against the Conemaugh Viaduct railroad bridge, which spanned the valley. The stream collapsed the viaduct within minutes, having built up new force from the volume of water that gathered during the moments the flood was halted.

The inexorable wall of water hit Johnstown around 4:10 p.m., traveling at some 40 m.p.h. and towering some 35 to 40 ft.- (10.6 to 12 m-) high in places. Trapped in the valley, the townspeople had no escape route. When the floodwaters receded, more than 2,200 people were dead, more than 700 of them so disfigured by their ordeal that they could not be identified. Some 1,600 homes were destroyed, and 4 sq. mi. of the city was devastated.

The recovery effort required years, and it brought forth a powerful new presence on the American scene. Among the first to arrive in the battered city was famed Civil War nurse Clara Barton, president of a relief organization she had founded only eight years before, the American Red Cross. Barton's tireless efforts to raise money and provide aid for the survivors of the disaster set strong standards of professionalism and created the model for a new era in the practice of organized rescue and relief operations.

Many accused the club owners of being complicit in the tragedy. Yet the primary deterioration of the South Fork Dam preceded their ownership of the structure, and the few lawsuits filed against the club owners were unsuccessful. The rains were an act of God; the failure of the dam can be blamed on the negligence of many men. ■

Fallacies and Fallout

March 28, 1979

The Three Mile Island accident shut down a nuclear future

THE COVER OF THE *TIME* MAGAZINE ISSUE for the week of April 9, 1979, fairly screamed its message—"Nuclear Nightmare"—after a reactor at the Three Mile Island plant near Harrisburg, Pa., partially melted down. Thirty-three years later, Americans of a certain age recognize Three Mile Island as shorthand for a nuclear crisis. The TMI accident was indeed a scary cultural moment, coming just two weeks after the release of the movie *The China Syndrome,* which frightened Americans with its depiction of an accident in a nuclear plant. But the TMI incident was not particularly tragic. There were no immediate deaths, although a 1996 study found lung cancer and leukemia rates were two to 10 times higher in downwind areas near the plant as opposed to upwind in the 10 years after the event. Nor did it kill nuclear power, which still provides 20% of U.S. electricity. It didn't even kill TMI; the plant's surviving reactor received a 20-year extension of its operating license in 2009. But it did shut down a nuclear future for the U.S.

What really happened at Three Mile Island? Because of a cooling malfunction, the core of one of the plant's two reactors partially melted down, releasing a small amount of radioactive matter into the atmosphere. Human error was the key problem, according to the Nuclear Regulatory Commission. An NRC investigation determined that the plant's operators overrode the automatic safety systems in their attempts to correct the rapidly developing crisis that occurred when an electricity-generating turbine tripped, or shut itself down. That response turned what should have been a minor glitch into a potential disaster.

Shaken by spectacular cost overruns, endless construction delays and public fury, the U.S. nuclear industry was already canceling new reactors all over the country before the 1979 incident, and no new ones have been ordered since. That's a shame, TIME's Michael Grunwald argued in 2009, because nuclear reactors produce no carbon emissions: the more nuclear power the U.S. uses, the less greenhouse gas we will pump into the atmosphere.

Today's nuclear industry is no longer dysfunctional. Its reactors are running at near capacity levels. It's doing a better job of storing its radioactive waste at its plants. It has standardized, safer designs for new reactors. But big problems remain: the government hasn't solved the problem of storing long-term waste; the cost of building new plants has skyrocketed; and the March 2011 meltdowns at the nuclear plant in Fukushima, Japan, have made the public once again deeply suspicious that nuclear plants can ever be shielded from major natural disasters such as tsunamis, tornadoes or earthquakes. Three decades after Three Mile Island, nuclear power is the Orson Welles of the U.S. energy industry, a story of spectacular potential wasted in part by self-inflicted wounds. ∎

Inside story *A worker checks Three Mile Island's Unit 1 reactor on March 28, 1979, the day that Unit 2, its twin, partially melted down. No deaths or injuries resulted, and Unit 2 has been shut down since the even*

Meltdown in Ukraine

April 26, 1986

A nuclear accident could haunt Chernobyl for 20 millenniums

THE RESIDENTS of Pripyat had no way of knowing that their small Ukrainian town was dying that morning as they gazed at the ruddy glow over Chernobyl reactor No. 4, some 2 miles (3 km) away. It was a sunny spring Saturday, and one resident came in from sunning himself on a roof, exclaiming that he had never seen anything like it: he

had turned brown in no time at all. The man had what would later be known as a nuclear tan. A few hours afterward, he was taken away in an ambulance, convulsed with uncontrollable vomiting. Soon many of his neighbors were coughing, throwing up and complaining of headaches and a metallic taste in their mouth.

During the night, in the worst nuclear power disaster ever, a catastrophic series of explosions had shattered the reactor, blowing the roof off the containment chamber. Firemen had extinguished the initial fire but could not quench the combustion of the molten core that was spewing 50 tons of radioactive isotopes into the atmosphere. Despite the beauty of the springtime scene, everything for miles around was drenched with lethal radiation.

The full story of the meltdown, hushed up for years by authorities, eventually emerged. While firefighters, engineers and others heroically exposed themselves to massive doses of radiation as they tried to contain the

damage, Chernobyl's bosses moaned, wrung their hands and did little else. Meanwhile, all night, as the reactor core blazed, local residents calmly fished in the cooling pond just outside, watching the spectacle, oblivious to the danger.

No one had any way of estimating how much radiation exposure the Chernobyl workers suffered, since all the measuring instruments at the plant had gone off the scale. Nor did Pripyat doctors know much about treating radiation sickness. The windows at the clinic were left open as the radioactive fire roared a few miles away. The fallout was wafting in like sunlight, settling over everything. The doctors themselves were being poisoned; patients were emanating radiation.

In retrospect, the accident is not surprising. According to the 1991 book *The Truth About Chernobyl,* by deputy plant engineer Grigori Medvedev, many key plant managers and technicians at Chernobyl knew nothing about nuclear technology. Patronage held sway over professionalism when it came to filling top jobs that carried prestige and good pay. The accident, ironically, occurred during a safety exercise, when incompetent managers exposed the core of reactor No. 4, depriving it of vital cooling water.

What Medvedev calls the "conspiracy of silence," which had cloaked the Soviet nuclear power program in secrecy and lies for 35 years, added to the human and

Accident and victim *This photo of the incinerated reactor, taken by Igor Kostin in 1986 shortly after the meltdown, alerted the world to the full impact of the event, which was being hushed up by authorities. Other images he took of the plant were over-exposed by radiation.*

At left, this photo of a young girl was taken in 1990. Birth deformities soared in the area after the disaster.

Emergency *Risking his life to document the tragedy, Romanian-born photographer Igor Kostin shot these workers being bused to the plant in May 1986. As of 2012, Kostin lives in Kiev, still takes photos of Chernobyl—and suffers from radiation poisoning*

environmental cost. In a country where nuclear accidents had never been reported, the pressure to cover up the monumental disaster at Chernobyl was enormous. Plant managers lied to government officials, insisting that the reactor was intact. Even as a radioactive cloud was spreading over thousands of square miles of Europe, Soviet bureaucrats were still denying the accident. At the same time, Moscow bosses quashed early requests by Chernobyl officials to evacuate the area, dooming many.

Experts agree there is little chance that a Chernobyl-type meltdown would occur at a U.S. plant. Since the U.S. has no reactors similar to Chernobyl in design, and because the accident resulted from a breathtaking level of ineptitude, ignorance and criminal negligence, Americans have little reason to fear a similar occurrence.

Today, the bleak region that surrounds the Chernobyl plant remains polluted; it is known as the "zone of alienation." Here, in a circle that extends 19 miles (30 km) in every direction, abandoned cars, tractors, buildings and homes are slowly being devoured by trees and shrubs. A classroom bulletin board not far from Lenin Street, in the center of Pripyat, where the plant workers used to live reads, "No return. Farewell, Pripyat. April 28, 1986."

In 2011, the 25th anniversary of the accident, TIME writers Eben Harrell and James Marson visited this eerie landscape, about 80 miles (50 km) from Kiev, the capital of Ukraine, and found that the effort to contain the Chernobyl accident is far from over: workers in white protective suits and respirator masks show up for work every day, constructing a new concrete shield to replace a massive sarcophagus built in 1986 that contains the still-radioactive core. The sarcophagus is starting to crumble and could collapse, which could release another radioactive cloud into the air. The 300 "worker ants" who bustle around the site are carefully monitored: they live outside the exclusion zone and labor no more than five hours a day for one month before taking 15 days of rest.

Chernobyl offers many lessons about what Princeton University engineering professor Robert Socolow calls the "afterheat" of a nuclear disaster, but it's the generational lesson that's most important. Because some of the isotopes released during a nuclear accident remain radioactive for tens of thousands of years, cleanup is the work not just of first responders but also of their descendants and their descendants' descendants. Asked when the reactor site may again become inhabitable, Ihor Gramot-

The wasteland *This aerial view of the city of Pripyat, taken in the 1990s, shows it largely abandoned. Under the laws governing the zone of alienation, no one lives in the region except a few residents at the time of the accident who have refused to leave*

kin, director of the Chernobyl power plant, replies, "At least 20,000 years."

That time scale is hard to grasp: How can safety measures be tracked over the course of millenniums? Already, the financing of cleanup and maintenance operations is proving difficult. On April 19, 2011, the Ukrainian government hosted an international donor conference in Kiev to raise money for the new $1.1 billion concrete shelter. The result fell some $300 million short of that goal, and Kiev is holding out for further pledges. It's sobering to think that the gigantic concrete shield—361 ft. (110 m) high and weighing 29,000 tons—has a woefully brief life when measured in radiological time: it will need to be replaced in a century unless the extremely radioactive core inside can be safely removed and stored somewhere else, itself an expensive and difficult operation. "Neither Ukraine nor the world community has the right to turn its back" on Chernobyl, Ukrainian President Viktor Yanukovych said at the end of the conference. "The accident left a deep wound that we will have to cope with for many years."

Everything to do with radiation moves at an insidiously slow pace. Exposure to radioactive particles increases the risk of cancer, but the level of the danger depends on the dose and the age and health of the affected population. When radiation does kill, it can still take years. Around Chernobyl, no accurate dosage estimates for the most heavily affected population were made until after the breakup of the Soviet Union; as a result, Belarus, Russia and Ukraine all use different techniques for measuring exposure. The International Agency for Research on Cancer has estimated that 16,000 cancer deaths in Europe through 2065 would not have happened but for Chernobyl. Because radiation spread beyond Europe to other areas in the northern hemisphere—Asia, Africa and the Americas —the Union of Concerned Scientists, a nonprofit watchdog, puts the global death toll closer to 27,000.

In the years following Chernobyl, some in the nuclear industry claimed such an accident would not happen again. Yet as of 2012, about 90,000 residents near Fukushima in northeast Japan had been evacuated from their homes after the March 2011 tsunami sent radioactive steam leaking from reactors at the nuclear plant there; they may never return. The afterheat of the Chernobyl accident offers a sobering reminder that the effects of radiation linger for generations. Radiation is, in the words of Princeton professor Socolow, "a fire that cannot be put out." ∎

Fukushima's Flaws

March 11, 2011

Japan's killer tsunami cripples a nuclear-power plant

THINK OF IT AS THE DOMINO THEORY OF disaster. On March 11, 2011, a giant undersea earthquake, measuring 9.0 in magnitude, shook the ocean floor some 80 mi. (129 km) off the northeastern shores of the Japanese archipelago. The quake moved a huge volume of water, creating a tsunami, Japanese for "great harbor wave." Like all tsunamis, this one barely registered on the surface of the ocean. But when it reached the shallow depths near Japan's coastline, it grew in power, coming ashore as a mighty surge, as high as 100 ft. (30 km) in places, that devastated everything in its path: automobiles, houses, stores, office buildings—and nuclear plants. At the city of Fukushima on the island of Honshu, the tsunami surge crashed into the Fukushima

Daiichi nuclear plant and shut down its power supply, leading to the complete meltdown of three of its six reactors and creating the planet's most significant nuclear disaster since the 1986 accident at Chernobyl in Ukraine.

The crisis at the Daiichi plant was principally a result of flooding, which inundated emergency power systems and made it impossible to pump needed cooling water to the fuel rods in the reactors. For plant engineers, too much water where they didn't want it resulted in too little where they did. So why didn't the Japanese prepare?

Actually, they did. About 40% of Japan's coastline is protected by seawalls, but near Fukushima, the 33 ft. (10 m) tsunami—a very big one—easily overtopped them. Still, simply because the region flooded didn't mean the plant's

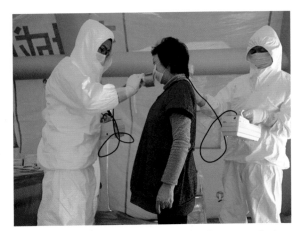

Japan's ordeal *At left, residents of Hirono, near Fukushima, don protective garments before returning to their homes inside the exclusion zone to retrieve personal items in June. Above left, the plant leaks radioactive steam on March 14. At right, a resident of Naraha, inside the exclusion zone, has her radiation level checked on March 16, five days after the tsunami hit the plant*

diesel-powered generators had to be swamped. Situating them above sea level could have kept them running. But since the designers assumed the seawall would be sufficient, they put the diesels on the ground floor of the plant. The quake caused grid power to be lost, and within an hour, the backup generators sputtered to a stop too.

A power-plant blackout is something safety experts train hardest for—and dread the most—because even the best nuclear reactors operate on a thermal knife edge. At Fukushima, even with coolant constantly bathing the fuel rods, the temperature inside the core stayed above 500°F (260°C). When the diesels died, the coolant pumps quit. In less than 24 hours, the temperature rose above 2,200°F (1,200°C). That caused the vessels to vent highly combustible hydrogen, which filled the buildings and led to a series of sequential explosions, which in turn released radioactive steam into the atmosphere: Reactor 1 the day after the quake, Reactor 3 two days later, Reactor 2 the day after that. On March 15, a new danger erupted, when Reactor 4 also suffered overheating and an explosion, even though it was not operating when the power went down.

In the first days of the crisis, Japan's government and plant managers dissembled about the extent of the danger, sending out false statements about the condition of the reactors. But as the extent of the radiation leakage became clear, the evacuation zone mandated by authorities kept expanding; it started at 1.9 miles (3 km), and by March 15 it stood at 18.6 miles (30 km).

Late in April, Japanese nuclear-safety officials, who had downplayed the accident's impact, finally raised their assessment of the crisis to Level 7, the highest ranking on an international scale of nuclear-incident severity, put-

ting the Fukushima disaster on par with the Chernobyl explosion. They also noted that the peak release of radiation had long passed: the rate had dropped 90% since the immediate aftermath of the tsunami. More good news: despite the new assessment, the Fukushima accident has released only about 10% as much radioactive material as Chernobyl did and should pose fewer health risks.

On Aug. 22 the government admitted that the levels of radioactive contamination might keep areas near the plant off-limits for human habitation for years, even decades. Said Chief Cabinet Secretary Yukio Edano: "There are areas near the nuclear power plant where the level of radiation is very high, and it cannot be denied that there may be areas where it will be difficult for the residents to return for a long time. I am very sorry for that." The 90,000 Japanese who had lived within the final exclusion zone, a 12.4-mile (20 km) radius of the plant, were liable to be a lot sorrier.

On Dec. 16, Japan's government declared that all the reactors had reached a state of "cold shutdown" and were no longer leaking significant amounts of radiation into the air. Ten days later, the government released an interim report on the crisis that condemned authorities' response to the accident, describing it as confused and littered with problems, including the failure to disclose the extent of the radiation leaks in timely fashion. Such delays unnecessarily exposed thousands near the plant to radiation. The final report is due in mid-2012, and it is likely to make difficult reading for Japan's government, for the operators of the Daiichi plant, for the exiled former residents of Fukushima and for the world's already beleaguered nuclear-power industry. ∎

On the Rocks

March 24, 1989

The *Exxon Valdez* crash creates a "constantly renewing disaster"

WANT TO FEEL LIKE A 19TH CENTURY prospector? Grab a shovel, kneel down on the stony beach on Knight Island, in Alaska's Prince William Sound, and start digging. The land around you is some of the most beautiful in the U.S. Snow-capped mountains, their flanks lush with hemlock and spruce, thrust out of the glacier-fed waters of the sound. Pale Arctic terns and endangered Kittlitz's murrelets skim the etched shoreline. To the northwest, fishing boats are setting out their gill nets, readying for the sockeye salmon's run. But as you turn your spade on the beach, chances are you will uncover a scar on the sound's pristine face: a pool of watery crude oil, chemical sheen glistening, soon fills in the hole.

Search elsewhere on the beach, and on other islands in the sound, and you'll find more oil, just beneath the surface: remnants of the crude spilled on March 24, 1989, by a tanker named *Exxon Valdez* that ran aground just after midnight while on its way out to sea with 53 million gal. (200 million L) of Alaskan oil on board. According to scientists from the National Oceanic and Atmospheric Administration, about 20,000 gal. (76,000 L) still remains buried on beaches around the sound. "At the initial time of the cleanup, we really thought this would be a one-shot

deal," Jeep Rice, the NOAA scientist who led a study of the accident, told TIME environment writer Bryan Walsh in 2009 as he stood on the beach, which was nicknamed Death Marsh during the cleanup. "We had no idea there would be lingering oil."

Then again, a lot of oil—and a lot of printer's ink—was spilled because of the accident. The *Exxon Valdez* spill was at the time considered to be the worst man-made environmental disaster in U.S. history, and news of it reverberated around the world. America's last true wilderness had been violated. At least 11 million gal. (42 million L) of crude bled into the water when the tanker struck Bligh Reef near the port town of Valdez, the terminus of the Trans Alaska Pipeline. For months after the grounding, large swaths of the sound and its islands were coated with a foul layer of crude. Hundreds of thousands of shorebirds were killed within weeks; a productive fishing industry was damaged for years.

The captain of the *Exxon Valdez*, Joseph Hazelwood, absent from the wheelhouse at the time of the accident, was tried on felony charges but convicted of a misdemeanor and fined $50,000. "It was a bad, bad time," Stan Stephens, a tour-boat operator in Valdez, told Walsh. "People can't even talk about it without getting emotional."

Deal with it *At left, the* Exxon Valdez *is towed to port. Above, workers hired by Exxon in the mammoth cleanup effort use pressure sprayers to clear crude oil from polluted beaches. Below, a worker attempts to remove oil from a shorebird*

TOP: BOB HALLINEN—ANCHORAGE DAILY NEWS—MCT VIA GETTY IMAGES; BOTTOM: JACK SMITH—AP IMAGES

The spill, it turns out, damaged more than Alaska's natural resources: it also afflicted the mental health of the nearby community. Alcoholism, domestic abuse, stress and divorce all skyrocketed in the wake of the disaster, and the wounds were slow to heal. One of the most surprising findings from research studies is that the biggest predictor of sustained stress years after the event wasn't whether victims were fishermen or lived close to the spill, but whether they were involved in a lawsuit.

Fighting Exxon in court led to what sociologist Steven Picou called a secondary disaster, as the lawsuits forced the victims to relive the accident over and over. A 2009 study found that levels of stress among those Alaskans who were involved in litigation over the oil spill were as high in 2009 as they were in 1991. The oil spill was, as Picou termed it, a "constantly renewing disaster."

Yet as shocking as the *Exxon Valdez* accident was, its long-term impact on the U.S. more than two decades later can seem all but invisible, like those last pockets of oil trapped beneath the beach. Although the Oil Pollution Act of 1990 passed in the accident's wake led to local improvements in shipping crude—like a mandatory shift to double-hulled tankers—spills still occur in the U.S., most recently in 2010, when an oil-rig explosion sent millions of gallons of crude pouring into the Gulf of Mexico.

Moreover, the root cause of the *Exxon Valdez* disaster

remains unaddressed. While the partial meltdown at the Three Mile Island power plant in 1979 curtailed the growth of the nuclear industry in the U.S., the Prince William Sound disaster did nothing to break the U.S. reliance on oil. In 2009, Americans were consuming 2 million more bbl. of oil a day than they did in 1989. "I was hoping for a huge shift in philosophy afterward," Riki Ott, a biologist and fisherman from the sound whose 2008 book on the spill is titled *Not One Drop,* told TIME's Walsh. "But it hasn't worked that way yet." ■

Patterns *Oil leaking from the blown-out Deepwater Horizon well creates abstract swirls around a boat in the waters of the Gulf of Mexico.*

In the inset photo at right, firefighting ships attempt to stop the fire at the oil rig

Oil Spill in the Gulf

April 20, 2010

The lessons of the Deepwater Horizon blowout

THE BIGGEST ENVIRONMENTAL DISASTER TO AFFLICT THE U.S. IN RECENT YEARS occurred on April 20, 2010—the 40th anniversary of Earth Day—when British Petroleum's Deepwater Horizon oil rig exploded in the Gulf of Mexico. The largest oil spill in U.S. history sent 4.9 million bbl. of crude pouring into the Gulf before the well was capped, and the crisis grabbed the public's imagination as no environmental story had since the *Exxon Valdez* oil spill in 1989. Underwater cameras revealed the daily failure of BP and the government to stop the flow of oil, while photographers captured oil-drenched beaches along the Gulf and animals slicked with crude. Here was the model of a modern environmental disaster: the failures of a huge multinational corporation would be visited on a highly localized environment, threatening the future of the enormous Gulf fishery and the livelihoods of tens of thousands of its workers, who bore no responsibility for the oil spill but would reap its woes.

Yet as TIME environment correspondent Bryan Walsh reported a year after the disaster took place, scientists were surprised to find that the Gulf had fared better than they had feared. Take the oil itself: scientists with the National Oceanic and Atmospheric Administration estimated in August 2010 that much of the spilled oil would remain in the Gulf, yet later independent studies verified that it had largely disappeared from the water. The savior of the Gulf, it turns out, was bacteria. Scientists from Lawrence Berkeley National Laboratory; University of California, Santa Barbara; and Texas A&M University traveled to the site of the blown well and found that microbes had digested much of the oil and methane that remained in the water. By autumn of 2010, oil levels were back to normal (some oil, leaking up through the seabed, is always present in Gulf waters). "It's very surprising it happened so fast," John Kessler, an oceanographer with Texas A&M, told Walsh. "It looks like natural systems can handle an event like this somewhat on their own."

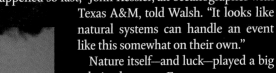

Nature itself—and luck—played a big role in the story. Fortunate ocean currents kept some of the oil from reaching shore, while increasing the flow of the Mississippi River provided more pushback. While parts of the southern Louisiana coast were hit hard by the oil, much of the Gulf Coast was spared. As a result, early indications suggest that the Gulf's fisheries seem to have escaped severe damage. A Texas A&M report estimated that the region's shrimp fisheries would rebound to normal within two years, although its oyster beds, which were severely damaged, might take up to a decade to recover.

That's a lot of good news for the Gulf. But hold the celebration: Walsh cautions that it is far too early to declare victory in this disaster, whose long-term effects have yet to play out. Yet the lessons learned in the Gulf may help scientists develop better bioremediation techniques to clean up the next major spill—because you can't always count on nature to heal itself. ∎

Hero's welcome *Below, miner Mario Gomez exits the Phoenix 2 capsule. At right, Chileans rally to support the miners in Copiapó*

Buried Alive

August 5–October 13, 2010

A deadly disaster is averted in Chile, as miners trapped underground for 69 days are freed

LEFT: MARTIN BERNETTI—AFP—GETTY IMAGES. RIGHT: MARIANA BAZO—REUTERS—LANDOV

BY THE TIME THE CAPSULE ROSE THROUGH THE MINE SHAFT'S MANHOLE-size opening shortly after midnight on Oct. 13, 2010, the desert outside the northern Chilean city of Copiapó was as dark and cold as a sepulcher. But when 30-year-old Florencio Avalos emerged from 2,300 ft. (700 m) below the earth and into the arms of his wife and children, an incandescent fiesta of life erupted on the surrounding dunes and rock piles. The miner and 32 companions had been huddled in solitude since their gold and copper mine collapsed on Aug. 5; now the men who had been all but buried alive for 69 days, as well as those who had rescued them, were becoming the world's newest heroes.

With the emergence of Avalos, Chile—and, for that matter, South America, a continent whose achievements are so often overshadowed by natural and political tragedy—celebrated its own finest hour as it rescued the 33 miners from the abyss. Chileans, not known for exuberance, unleashed deafening cheers and chants through the chilly air above the San José mine—"Tonight we bring them back!"—along with confetti and balloons bearing the Chilean flag. The sight of Avalos' 7-year-old son, wearing a hard hat and standing beside Chilean President Sebastián Piñera as he awaited his father, brought tears to many at Camp Hope, the rescue station set up at the mine.

"We made a promise to never surrender, and we kept it," said Piñera, who arrived at the site, about 530 miles (850 km) north of Santiago, Chile's capital, the day before the rescue began. Earlier, he had said that the miners' rescue would be "a true rebirth for us all." That rebirth, capping a survival record in the annals of mining disasters, became a prolonged celebration that transfixed a

Greetings *A miner, with shirt off, hugs Manuel Gonzalez, the first rescue worker to arrive at the men's refuge some 2,300 ft. (700 m) under the ground. Additional paramedics and rescue workers made the journey to the bunker during the operation*

Life preserver *The Phoenix 2 capsule is shown suspended from the crane used to winch it up and down the hole bored into the men's bunker. The capsule itself was only 21 in. (53 cm) wide; the vehicle was lifted to the surface at a rate of 3.3 ft. (1 m) each second*

vast global audience. Indeed the profound emotions generated by Operation San Lorenzo, named for the patron saint of miners, seemed to grow rather than diminish as each resurrected miner reached the surface.

The process of sending the 21-in. (53 cm) -wide capsule down the almost half-mile (.8 km) diagonal duct and then carrying each miner up to the surface initially took about an hour for each rescue, then sped up. It ended some 22 hours later, when the last man emerged from the tunnel: Luis Urzúa, 52, the shift foreman who was the men's leader and kept them cohesive during their ordeal, a role he played throughout the rescue phase as well. Urzúa kept a straight face as he declared, "It's been a bit of a long shift."

When Urzúa placed his foot on the ground, it brought an end to an ordeal that began in early August, when the mine collapsed and the world feared the miners had been lost. But far below, the men were alive, gathered in a shelter measuring about 500 sq. ft. (45 sq m), no larger than a small studio apartment. With Urzúa in charge, they ate sparingly of rations intended to last for only 48 hours, eating two teaspoons of tuna and one biscuit every two days, washing down their "meals" with a small sip of milk. The meager rations helped keep them going for an incredible 17 days until the outside world learned the good news: against the odds, all 33 miners were still alive.

"Estamos bien en el refugio, los 33," they wrote in a note attached to the end of a probe that bored into the shelter on Aug. 22. "We are well inside the shelter, the 33." Those first words came after several attempts to drill down and

reach any surviving miners had failed, primarily because of inaccurate maps. In those first moments after they were discovered, the men peered eagerly into a miniature camera, their eyes blazing with euphoria. Among the first requests: toothbrushes. Later, a second bore hole was driven into the cavern; the 6-in. (15 cm) portal served as an umbilical cord through which food, water, oxygen capsules, glucose and rehydration tablets reached the waiting men. As hope of a rescue soared, miner Mario Sepúlveda, a.k.a. "Super Mario," began sending video logs of the men's ordeal to the watching world.

The final phase of the rescue operation began on Oct. 9, when a giant U.S.-operated drill managed to bore a man-sized hole through the ceiling of the refuge, a good month before most rescue officials had expected. The hole was large enough to fit a capsule, christened Phoenix 2, specially designed by the Chilean navy in collaboration with NASA. (Three capsules were built and tested; Phoenix 2 was chosen as the rescue vehicle.)

The men prepared for their ascent by doing exercises assigned by doctors. On the trip, each wore a special helmet equipped with communications gear so officials could keep in constant contact as well as a belt with vital-signs sensors around the torso. The ascending miners also wore dark glasses to keep their eyes, now more like those of moles than of humans, from being damaged in the glare of light, whether from the sun or from the giant batteries of floodlights that surrounded the surface camp at night, upon their arrival.

Home again *Miner Claudio Yanez applauds his rescuers as he is carried to the temporary medical facility erected near the rescue operation, where the men were first examined before being sent to a hospital in Copiapó. None required emergency treatment*

A problem with the capsule door delayed the operation's start, but Manuel Gonzalez, the first of a handful of rescue workers to descend into the sanctuary, was lowered down shortly after 11 p.m. to gauge the miners' condition and assist them with the capsule. Within minutes Avalos, the No. 2 leader of the mining group, who had helped monitor his comrades' health for officials above, was on his way up.

The ascents required about 15 minutes each, and the rescue operation ran for about 22 hours all told. Each miner was allowed to have about three family members greet him as he popped through the hole, then was examined by doctors at a makeshift medical facility at the rescue site. Then each man was whisked by helicopter to a hospital in Copiapó for a minimum of two days' observation. Below the ground, rescuers who had assisted in the operation held up a sign reading MISIÓN CUMPLIDA CHILE ("Mission Accomplished Chile"). Their exuberant gesture was seen live by an estimated 1 billion people around the world.

Up top, a relieved Margarita Rojo, 72, the mother of miner Dario Segovia, 48, admitted to TIME that she had feared the rescue would take longer. Then again, she said, she had been a miner herself as a younger woman, an explosives expert to boot. Her son, she said, "is a miner—they're like cats, with nine lives. He's got three or four left at least." For the two days of Operation San Lorenzo, such expressions of hope lit up the watching world as surely as they illuminated the barren Chilean desert. ■

Ten Deadliest Coal-Mining Disasters in U.S. History

■ An explosion in 1907 that killed 362 miners in Monongah, W.Va., led directly to the formation of the U.S. Bureau of Mines, and decades of government regulation have succeeded in mitigating many of the dangers of mining. Yet some mine operators continue to flout safety codes, as was the case in the explosion in the Upper Big Branch Mine in West Virginia on April 5, 2010, that killed 29 people.

Coal is heavily mined in the U.S., and coal-mine disasters have accounted for most mining fatalities, although 163 workers died in 1917 when fire raged through the Granite Mountain Shaft, a copper mine in Butte, Mont.

LOCATION, YEAR	DEATHS
Monongah, W.Va. (1907)	362
Dawson, N.M. (1913)	263
Cherry, Ill. (1909)	259
West Frankfurt, Ill. (1951)	119
Centralia, Ill. (1947)	111
Bartley, W.Va. (1940)	91
Farmington, W.Va. (1968)	78
St. Clairsville, Ohio (1940)	72
Hyden, Ky. (1970)	38
Montcoal, W.Va. (2010)	29

Memorial *Mourners grieve at a commemorative service after the deaths of 29 workers at the Upper Big Branch Mine in Montcoal, W.V., in 2010*

A Silent Cloud of Death

December 2-3, 1984

An industrial gas leak kills thousands in India

LOOKING BACK 20 YEARS, IT WAS THE NIGHT her husband Kishen Chand went blind that she first saw life's woes clearly, Shanti Debi told TIME in 2004. Awakened by her daughter's cries that she was suffocating, Shanti thought she could smell burning chilies. The next moment, everyone in the family was taken violently ill, and Kishen lost his sight. Right then, Shanti's life began to disintegrate, along with the social fabric of her hometown, Bhopal, capital of India's state of Madhya Pradesh. "Everybody just rushed out," she said. "Nobody cared about anybody else. I even left my own

children. Everybody just cared about saving their own life."

On the night of Dec. 2-3, 1984, Bhopal suffered one of the worst industrial accidents of modern times. On the edge of town stood a 172-acre pesticide plant co-owned by the U.S. company Union Carbide. Around midnight, water passed through a safety valve that had been deactivated and poured into a 42-ft. (13 m) steel tank of methyl isocyanate (MIC), a chemical used in many pesticides. The water caused a superheated reaction, turning the MIC into a deadly gas. Then the tank ruptured, breaking clean through its concrete housing, and 27 tons of MIC

Aftermath *At left, survivors of the gas leak gather in a "widows' colony" in Bhopal. Above, a survivor carries his wife's body to a collection station. In the distance is the Union Carbide plant, source of the gas leak that claimed more than 15,000 lives*

was released into the atmosphere. Over the next weeks, months and years, Kishen and 15,247 others died—often blinded and poisoned or drowned as the gas turned to liquid in their lungs—and a further 572,173 out of a population that was then 900,000 needed treatment.

In the years since the disaster, the survivors have seen a more insidious venom spread across the town. Without a healthy work force, the economy stagnated as businesses and factories such as Kishen's ice-cream factory, which had paid for a five-bedroom house and three servants, closed overnight. Replacing them was an army of quack healers, fly-by-night nongovernmental organizations and lawyers on the make. After fighting compensation claims in the courts for five years, Union Carbide paid out $470 million, but families of victims often received only $500 for injuries and $2,000 for deaths.

The tragedy at Bhopal introduced the world to a new form of disaster, TIME's Roger Rosenblatt argued in 1984. "The industrialized society has created a shared fragility," he wrote. "The sources of enhancement are also the sources of fear and peril—all the chemical plants, nuclear power plants and other strangely shaped structures concocting potential salvation and destruction in remote and quiet places. The citizens of Bhopal lived near the Union Carbide plant because they sought to live there. The plant provided jobs, the pesticide more food. Bhopal was a modern parable of the risks and rewards originally engendered by the Industrial Revolution: Frankenstein's wonder becoming Frankenstein's monster."

For Shanti, 60 years old when she spoke to TIME in 2004, the past 20 years have revealed the frailty of community. "After Kishen died, I faced a lot of problems. So did a lot of families. But … I was never begging for money. I was begging for love. And Bhopal had none." ∎

Disasters
IN SPACE

Out of place *Residents of Nacogdoches, Texas, were startled to find objects falling from the sky on Feb. 1, 2003, as the breakup of the space shuttle* Columbia *scattered a trail of debris, like this hydrogen tank, across Texas, Arkansas and Louisiana*

STEVE LISS

Farewell to the *Challenger*

January 28, 1986

The space shuttle explodes on liftoff, claiming the lives
of six astronauts and a schoolteacher

Calamity *The space shuttle explodes in flames 73 sec. after liftoff, left. At right, spectators in the stands react to the disaster*

W HERE IN HELL IS THE BIRD? Where is the bird?" shouted an engineer at Cape Canaveral. "Oh, my God!" cried a teacher from the observation stands nearby. "Don't let happen what I think just happened." Nancy Reagan, watching television in the White House family quarters, gasped similar words, "Oh, my God, no!" So too did William Graham, the acting Administrator of NASA, who was watching in the office of a Congressman. "Oh, my God," he said. "Oh, my God."

Across the nation, people groped for words. "It exploded," murmured Brian French, a senior at Concord High School in New Hampshire, as the noisy auditorium fell quiet. A classmate, Kathy Gilbert, turned to him and asked, "Is that really where she was?" At the Jet Propulsion Laboratory in Pasadena, Calif., scientists turned away from their remarkable new photographs of the distant planet Uranus and stared, stunned, at the telecast from Florida. "We all knew it could happen one day," said one, "but, God, who would have believed it?"

It had happened. In one fiery instant, the U.S. public's complacent attitude toward manned space flight had evaporated at the incredible sight in the skies over Cape Canaveral. Americans had soared into space 55 times over 25 years, and their safe return had come to be taken for granted. An age when most anyone, given a few months' training, could go along for a safe ride seemed imminent.

Volunteer *New Hampshire schoolteacher Christa McAuliffe practiced flying weightless on a NASA training flight. She was selected from among 11,000 applicants to be the first U.S. teacher in space. Many schoolchildren watched* Challenger's *fatal liftoff live because of her participation in the mission*

Christa McAuliffe, 37, was the pioneer and the vibrant symbol of this amazing new era of space for Everyman. An ebullient high school social-studies teacher from Concord, N.H., she was to be the first ordinary citizen to be shot into space, charged with showing millions of watchful schoolchildren how wonderful it could be. She was bringing every American who had ever been taught by a Mrs. McAuliffe into this new era with her. It was an era that lasted only 73 sec.

The preparation for *Challenger's* 10th journey into space had been painstakingly careful, and for its crew, agonizingly slow. It was an aptly all-American group. There were two women, McAuliffe and Judith Resnik. Joining them were an African-American man, Ronald E. McNair; a Hawaiian of Japanese descent, Ellison S. Onizuka; and three white men, mission commander Francis R. Scobee, Gregory B. Jarvis and Michael J. Smith. The mission had originally been scheduled to lift off Jan. 20. The date slipped to Saturday, Jan. 25, after one of the other three space shuttles, *Columbia,* ran into delays with a mission that got relatively little notice because such flights had seemed so routine. Then it slipped again.

McAuliffe and her six crewmates were indeed ready, but the weather was not. A cold front was moving down the Florida peninsula, pushing a few showers ahead of it. On the night of Jan. 27, temperatures fell to an unseasonable 27 degrees, but the wind dwindled to 9 m.p.h. Finally, on Tuesday, Jan. 28, the clear morning sky formed what glider pilots fondly call "a blue bowl." Thousands of motorists in the cape area, listening to their radios, pulled off highways and faced the ocean for the countdown:

T minus 10 ... nine ... eight ... seven ... six ... We have main-engine start. Four ... three ... two ... one ... And liftoff. Liftoff of the 25th space shuttle mission. And it has cleared the tower.

Like runners passing a baton, NASA's Hugh Harris, who had narrated the countdown in Florida, handed off the public announcements to Steve Nesbitt, the communicator at the Johnson Space Center in Houston. At the cape, Nesbitt's voice was lost amid the cheers of some 1,000 spectators watching on bleachers some 4 mi. (6.4 km) from Pad 39B. Even at that distance, they could feel the punch of the blastoff; its power thrilled the crowd. A graceful sculpture arising from an explosion: it was just as it was supposed to look.

Among the relieved viewers were relatives of most of *Challenger's* crew, including McAuliffe's parents and her husband Steven. At Concord High School, back in New Hampshire, students who had gathered in the auditorium finally had a chance to blow their party horns and cheer their teacher's loftiest achievement.

NASA's long-range television cameras had been following *Challenger's* white rocket plume, recording the graceful roll that had awed the spectators. But then the cameras caught an ominously unfamiliar sight, imperceptible to those below. However different those photographs later looked to viewers of the endless taped replays, NASA analysts said that an orange glow had first flickered just past the center of the orbiter, between the shuttle's belly and the adjacent external tank. This was near the point where the tank is attached to *Challenger.* Milliseconds later, the fire had flared out and danced upward. Suddenly, there was only a fireball. Piercing shades of orange and yellow and red burst out of a billowing white cloud, engulfing the disintegrating spacecraft.

Snaking wildly out of control, the two booster rockets emerged from the conflagration, both clearly intact. They veered widely apart, leaving yellow-orange exhaust glows and gleaming white trails behind them. The configuration resembled a giant monster in the sky, its two claws reaching frantically forward.

In Houston, commentator Nesbitt had kept his eyes on the programmed flight data displayed in front of him, not yet aware of the images of disaster appearing on the TV monitor to his left. He reported what normally would have been the readings from *Challenger.* "One minute, 15 seconds. Velocity: 2,900 feet per second. Altitude: nine nautical miles. Downrange distance: seven nautical miles." To millions watching their own screens, Nesbitt's narration was surreal: they had seen the fireball. There was a 40-sec. pause and silence on the screen as viewers stared in baffled horror. Then, his voice still calm, Nesbitt announced, "Flight controllers are looking very carefully at the situation." He added quickly, "Obviously, a major malfunction." His unemotional tone did not change. Communications with the craft had been severed, he continued. "We have no downlink."

On the consoles in front of Nesbitt and the rows of technicians on duty in Houston, a series of S's froze on the monitoring screens. They signaled "static." No data readings were coming from *Challenger.* The range safety officer at the cape pressed a button to destroy the two boosters by radio. After another pause of 40 sec., Nesbitt pronounced the fateful verdict: "We have a report from the flight-dynamics officer that the vehicle has exploded. The flight director confirms that."

Disbelief turned to horror as the reality became all too clear: McAuliffe and six astronauts had disappeared in an orange-and-white fireball 9 mi. (14.4 km) above the Atlantic Ocean. So too had the space shuttle *Challenger,* the trusted $1.2 billion workhorse on which they had been riding. Transfixed by the terrible sight of the explosion, Americans watched as it was replayed again and again. And yet again. Communal witnesses to tragedy, they were bound, mostly in silence, by a nightmarish image, a scrawl of smoke and flame in the sky, destined to linger in the nation's shared consciousness.

Then the national mood shifted. America wept. From the White House to farmhouses, Americans joined in mourning their common loss. Flags were lowered to half-staff. Makeshift signs appeared in countless cities: WE SALUTE OUR HEROES. GOD BLESS THEM ALL. President Ronald Reagan, in a moving broadcast that afternoon, paraphrased a sonnet written by John Gillespie Magee Jr., a young American airman killed in World War II: "We will never forget them nor the last time we saw them this morning as they prepared for their journey and waved goodbye and 'slipped the surly bonds of earth to touch the face of God.'" That Friday night, all along the Florida coast, from Jacksonville to Miami, some 20,000 people pointed flashlights skyward in tribute to the deceased. ■

BETTMANN CORBIS

Behind the Disaster

■ Shocked by the destruction of the *Challenger,* NASA ordered an immediate end to all shuttle flights and President Reagan quickly appointed a commission, led by former Secretary of State William Rogers, to investigate the crash. Within days of the disaster, NASA had identified the problem: two O-rings, rubber seals on one of *Challenger'*s two solid rocket boosters, had failed. The commission also discovered that NASA itself was deeply flawed. Before the first shuttle was launched, the agency had known of the fatal seal problem but had buried it under a blizzard of paper while permitting schedule-conscious managers to keep the orbiters flying.

The accident began in the right booster rocket's O-rings, synthetic-rubber circles, 0.28 in. (0.7 cm) thick and 37.5 ft. (11.4 m) in circumference. The seals were designed to prevent the superhot gases generated within each solid booster from escaping through the joints of the rocket's segments. When flames did penetrate the booster, they ignited the shuttle's external liquid-fuel tank, causing the explosion.

To their dismay, committee members learned that the seals had long been flagged as a problem that could be aggravated by low temperatures, like those experienced in Florida on the morning of Jan. 28. Yet even so, NASA managers and supervisors at Morton Thiokol, the Utah-based builder of the boosters, overrode the warnings of Thiokol engineers in a teleconference the night before the liftoff. Four Thiokol vice presidents at first agreed with the engineers in opposing a cold-weather launch but when NASA executives disagreed, they took a "management vote" that excluded the engineers. NASA won the argument—and seven people aboard *Challenger* lost their lives.

The highlight of the inquiry came when the eminent physicist and commission member Richard Feynman, below, dropped a small version

of an O-ring into a glass of cold water to demonstrate how its properties changed under low temperatures. With this elegant, simple experiment, he proved his point: "For a successful technology, reality must take precedence over public relations, for Nature cannot be fooled."

97

Fatal flaw *A small, triangular piece of foam insulation, circled above, broke off during the launch and damaged the shuttle's wing*

Columbia

United States

A Flawed Launch
Leads to Disaster

Feb. 1, 2003

The space shuttle *Columbia* disintegrates on re-entry

THE LAST SONG THE LOST CREW OF THE SPACE SHUTTLE *COLUMBIA* EVER HEARD was *Scotland the Brave* by the 51st Highland Brigade. That was the wake-up song beamed up by NASA on the morning the ship was supposed to return to Earth. The day before it had been *Shalom Lach Eretz Nehederet,* for Israeli astronaut Ilan Ramon. Thursday morning it had been John Lennon's *Imagine. Scotland the Brave* was for mission specialist Laurel Clark, Scottish by extraction.

"Good morning," Mission Control called up to the ship. "Good morning, Houston," Clark answered. "We're getting ready for our big day up here … I'm really excited to come back home. Hearing that song reminds me of all the different places down on Earth and all the friends and family that I have all over the world." She had reason to be excited, particularly since that business of coming home should have been relatively routine—at least by the high-wire standards of space travel. After

Evidence *Scorched tiles from the skin of* Columbia *were located on the ground in Nacogdoches, Texas*

shimmying out of their sleep restraints, the crew would stow gear and belt themselves into their seats—a six-hour process. With *Columbia* turned rump forward, Mission Commander Rick Husband and pilot William McCool would then fire the main maneuvering engines, slowing the spacecraft and easing it toward the upper wisps of the atmosphere. They would then surf the currents of the thickening air, fishtailing this way and that until, just an hour or so after the deorbit engines were lit, *Columbia's* tires would make their smoking contact with the runway in Florida and the shuttle would come to a rolling stop.

That's the way it ought to have happened, at least—and that's the way it did happen on 111 of 112 earlier shuttle flights, 27 of them by the venerable *Columbia.* But only 16

minutes from its planned touchdown, more than 200,000 ft. (61,000 m) over Texas, the 22-year-old ship suddenly and fatally broke apart and disintegrated, leaving a stream of bright, shining trails across the sky and taking the lives of its seven crew members with it.

In Nacogdoches, Texas, 17-year-old Heath Drewery was in bed when he was jolted by what sounded like an explosion outside his house. "I heard this big rumble and thought a train had derailed," he said. He and his brother piled into their truck and drove into town, where the street was littered with debris. "There were pieces all over the place. It looked like it was charcoal," he declared.

As with NASA's *Challenger* disaster seventeen years before, an independent committee was formed to investigate

Fragments and heroes *At left, pieces of the shuttle retrieved during the extensive search that followed the breakup are placed in a hangar at the Kennedy Space Center.*

Above, the astronauts pose during the flight. In blue in the top row, left to right, are: David Brown, William McCool and Michael Anderson. In red, below: India's Kalpana Chawla, Rick Husband, Laurel Clark and Israel's Ilan Ramon

the reasons for the catastrophe. The breakup of the craft had created an enormous debris field that stretched across Texas and into Louisiana and southwestern Arkansas. Seeking clues, the U.S. government launched an immense ground search to locate the parts of the craft.

But as it turned out, the problem that doomed the ship had been evident from the beginning of the mission. According to the committee's Aug. 26, 2003, report, at the moment of launch, a piece of foam had broken away from the insulation on the rocket's giant external fuel tank and struck the left wing of the ship, damaging several of the 24,000 heat-absorbing black-and-white ceramic tiles that make up the skin of the ship and protect it from the hellish heat of re-entry. The breach in the left wing led directly to the overheating and eventual breakup of *Columbia.*

The committee of inquiry also learned that NASA engineers had been aware of the dangers posed by the damaged tiles from early in the mission, but top managers had rejected emergency measures recommended by some within the agency during the craft's 16 days in space, including using the International Space Station as a refuge for the astronauts until a rescue mission could be launched, or having one of the shuttle astronauts conduct a spacewalk to examine the craft's damaged wing. The committee's report strongly criticized NASA's internal policies and culture, which, it found, stressed compromising safety standards in order to achieve successful missions, no matter the danger to astronauts. The *Columbia* disaster was the beginning of the end for the shuttle program. Flights were suspended for more than two years; when they resumed, all missions except one flew only to the International Space Station, where the craft was examined for any tile flaws before returning to Earth. On July 21, 2011, the shuttle *Atlantis* landed safely in Cape Canaveral, ending the shuttle program's mission of exploration after 30 years, 133 successful flights—and two terrible disasters that claimed 14 lives. ■

Lost in Space

April 11-17, 1970

Facing death far from Earth, the Apollo 13 astronauts and
engineers on the ground improvise a solution that saves three lives

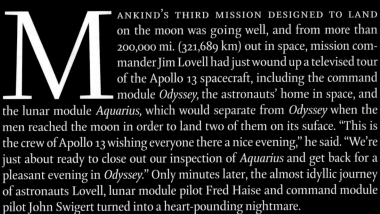

M ANKIND'S THIRD MISSION DESIGNED TO LAND on the moon was going well, and from more than 200,000 mi. (321,689 km) out in space, mission commander Jim Lovell had just wound up a televised tour of the Apollo 13 spacecraft, including the command module *Odyssey,* the astronauts' home in space, and the lunar module *Aquarius,* which would separate from *Odyssey* when the men reached the moon in order to land two of them on its suface. "This is the crew of Apollo 13 wishing everyone there a nice evening," he said. "We're just about ready to close out our inspection of *Aquarius* and get back for a pleasant evening in *Odyssey.*" Only minutes later, the almost idyllic journey of astronauts Lovell, lunar module pilot Fred Haise and command module pilot John Swigert turned into a heart-pounding nightmare.

Interrupting a conversation between Swigert and a ground controller at the Manned Spacecraft Center in Houston, Lovell suddenly said in a laconic voice, "Hey, Houston, we've had a problem here." It was the understatement of the space age. *Odyssey* had been rocked by "a pretty large bang" from its attached service module, which housed the spacecraft's main engine as well as most of its life-giving power and environmental systems. Almost immediately, *Odyssey's* instruments recorded a surge of electrical current followed by an alarming drop, as red and yellow warning lights flashed on. In Houston, controllers snapped to attention as telemetered data from Apollo 13 began to confirm the extent of the problem.

In less than a minute, one of the service module's two spherical oxygen tanks was completely empty; nearly 320 lbs. of supercold (-297°F, -183°C) oxygen, a highly pressurized mix of gas and liquid, had gushed out of the spacecraft through a rupture in its thin alloy skin. Looking out a window, Lovell saw vapor streaming by. "We are venting something into space," he reported. "It's a gas of some sort." At the same time, the spacecraft began to pitch and roll in reaction to the violent expulsion of the gas.

There was more trouble to come. "One of the main electrical circuits is lifeless," Swigert radioed. "It's off. It's dead." The mysterious blast had also affected two of the service module's three fuel cells, which produced the bulk of *Odyssey's* vital electrical power. It quickly became obvious that a moon landing was now out of the question; mission rules forbade a lunar landing if even one fuel cell became inoperative. The loss of two required the earliest possible

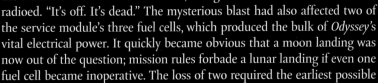

Jettisoned *At left, the damaged service module that provided support for the command module* Odyssey *drifts off into space after the astronauts separated it from* Odyssey. *At right, astronaut Fred Haise smiles during the mission*

Earthbound *Families of the astronauts gather in prayer in Houston as the crisis unfolds. The* Odyssey *command module landed in the South Pacific off the island of Samoa, where the astronauts were plucked to safety by a U.S. Navy helicopter, above*

return to Earth. Even worse, the second oxygen tank was now also rapidly losing its precious cargo. Unless the venting could be stopped, ground controllers calculated, *Odyssey* would be completely dead and uninhabitable in about 91 min. Without the least indication of panic, the astronauts prepared to take shelter in the lunar module *Aquarius*. The small, spindly craft had been designed primarily to land two men on the moon, sustain them there for two days or so and then carry them back to an orbital rendezvous with the command module. Now, if all went well, it would serve as the mission's lifeboat.

At the Manned Spacecraft Center, there was an air of tension and foreboding. The crippled spacecraft was now about 207,000 miles from home and still speeding toward the moon. Under the best of circumstances, it would take days—not minutes or hours—for the astronauts to return to the safety of Earth. Said no-nonsense Chris Kraft, the center's deputy director, in a candid briefing to newsmen: "This is as serious a situation as we've ever had in manned spaceflight." As he spoke, no one really knew what had caused the spacecraft's massive failure. A later investigation found that a short circuit inside one of the two oxygen tanks in *Odyssey's* service module had sparked the explosion.

In Houston, as news of the explosion spread, the astronauts' families and friends gathered to share prayers, while Americans, joined by a vast world audience, turned their eyes to the sky, bound in unity by the faraway crisis.

Aboard *Odyssey,* the astronauts remained remarkably cool. Lovell and Haise drifted through the darkened tunnel connecting the command ship with the lunar lander. While they powered up *Aquarius,* Swigert battened down

Odyssey; the command module had enough spare power for six hours of working life—enough time for the craft to re-enter the atmosphere and splash down in the ocean.

Aquarius hummed to life, but mission planners were still faced agonizing decisions. How could they best bring the distressed spacecraft home as quickly as possible but with a minimum of risk? *Odyssey's* big propulsion engine, in its service module, was powerful enough to turn it in midflight, but Houston was reluctant to try using it. Finally, the engineers gambled: they fired *Aquarius'* descent engine for 30.7 sec., putting the spacecraft on a course to round the moon and drop the astronauts in the South Pacific about 600 mi. (966 km) southeast of Samoa.

Inside the darkened spacecraft, the astronauts struggled to make the best of their dangerous predicament. While two slept fitfully in the unpowered and chilly command module, the third remained on watch "downstairs" in the lunar module. In the hours that followed, the three men circled the moon, but they never came closer than 158 mi. (254 km.) to its surface. As they emerged from behind its far side, they prepared for the crucial "hurry home" burn. But there was a hitch. So much debris was still floating outside the lunar module's windows that a star sighting—to align *Aquarius* properly for the burn—was impossible. So the spacemen neatly improvised, taking rough fixes on the moon and the sun. Then they fired *Aquarius'* descent engine, increasing the spacecraft's speed by 600 m.p.h. The 4-min. 24-sec. burn was so accurate that only two more small course corrections were subsequently needed.

For the first time in long hours, the tired men in Mission Control breathed easier. But the astronauts did not.

Safe! *Astronauts Haise, Swigert and Lovell (from left) celebrate on the U.S.S.* Iwo Jima. *At the same time, NASA engineers, who worked miracles of improvisation to save the men, celebrate at the Manned Spacecraft Center in Houston*

Houston soon noticed that carbon dioxide exhaled by the astronauts was building up to a dangerous level in the lunar module's atmosphere; air purifiers in *Aquarius,* designed to absorb the potentially lethal gas for only relatively short periods of time, were becoming saturated. Mission Control instructed the astronauts to lead a second hose into the command module and connect it to the canisters. Leaving nothing to chance, the astronauts stuffed a sock in the connection to make sure it was snug.

With its normal heat-producing systems shut off to conserve electricity, *Odyssey's* temperature dropped to nearly 40°F (4°C). On their last night in space, the astronauts donned two pairs of thermal underwear apiece to ward off the chill; Lovell even put on his bulky moon-walking shoes to keep his toes warm. Picking up speed under the increasing pull of Earth's gravity, Apollo was now rapidly approaching its narrow re-entry slot. To make sure of a precise re-entry, Lovell and Haise fired one more brief burst from *Aquarius'* thrusters.

A few minutes later, the men separated the spacecraft. Again hitting the thrusters, Lovell forced *Aquarius* against the command and service modules. Almost simultaneously, Swigert fired several explosive bolts, detaching the service module from *Odyssey.* Lovell then fired *Aquarius's* thrusters again. The "push-pull" tactic shoved the service module away from *Aquarius* and *Odyssey,* enabling the astronauts to see the disabled module for the first time. It was an incredible sight. The module had lost an entire 15-ft. (4.5 m) -long panel covering Bay 4, and a tangle of wiring and debris trailed out of the gaping hole. The astronauts photographed the damage; because the service module would burn up on re-entry, the pictures would be

important in determining the cause of the blast. "It's really a mess," Lovell told Mission Control. "Well, James," Houston answered, "if you can't take any better care of the spacecraft than that, we might not give you another."

About 30,000 mi. (48,280 km) from Earth, the astronauts climbed into *Odyssey,* sealed the hatch shut and exploded the small bolts connecting the command module with the lunar module. The *Aquarius* drifted rapidly away, its lifeboat function reliably and amply fulfilled. For 3 min. 38 sec., with radio contact down, the world anxiously waited to learn whether the astronauts had survived the final portion of their perilous voyage. Finally, the descending spaceship hove into view of the TV cameras on the aircraft carrier U.S.S. *Iwo Jima's* decks, about 4 mi. (6.4 km) away. Under billowing white-and-orange main chutes, the spacecraft drifted slowly downward, headed for a splashdown just off target. At exactly 1:08 p.m. on April 17, six days after its ill-starred journey began, *Odyssey's* wanderings had come to an end.

Forty-five minutes later, a helicopter ferried the three astronauts to the *Iwo Jima.* Smiling and remarkably steady on their feet, the astronauts were greeted by cheers from sailors. Doctors found them in surprisingly good health after their exhausting and agonizing adventure.

In Houston, cheering and applauding flight controllers joyously lit up their customary cigars as a heartfelt message flashed on a big screen: WELCOME BACK. An especially apt comment came from J. Leonard Swigert, the astronaut's father. Sipping champagne with reporters in his Denver home, the 67-year-old doctor said, "It was a wonderful beginning and a beautiful landing. But I wouldn't give you two hoots for the interim." ∎

Heroes *From left, Apollo 1 astronauts Grissom, White and Chaffee*

Death on the Launchpad

January 27, 1967

Three U.S. astronauts perish in a fire on the ground

AMERICANS RECALL NASA'S APOLLO PROGRAM, which put humans on the moon, with pride. But the triumphs of the program have overshadowed a memory that should be preserved, the deaths in a launchpad fire of the crew of Apollo 1: space veterans Gus Grissom and Ed White and their rookie colleague, Roger Chaffee. They died on Jan. 27, 1967, 19 years and one day before another NASA tragedy, when the *Challenger* shuttle exploded shortly after liftoff.

It was a Friday evening. Grissom, White and Chaffee were running through a simulated countdown on the pad at Cape Canaveral. They were fully suited, the capsule was fully pressurized, and the hatch was bolted shut. A frayed wire to Grissom's left let fly a spark, one that would have been harmless at sea level pressure in an ordinary nitrogen-oxygen atmosphere. In the high-pressure, 100% oxygen environment of the Apollo capsule, it was like dropping a match into a gas tank. A flash fire tore through the cockpit at temperatures exceeding 1,200°F (650°C), hot enough to ignite aluminum. Grissom, White and Chaffee tried to unbolt the hatch, but they were quickly overcome.

Grissom was a pioneer, a two-time space veteran who was the second American in space and commanded the first Gemini mission. White was a skywalker, the first American to leave his spacecraft and float tethered in the void above the planet. Chaffee was a fighter, a naval pilot who, before joining NASA, was flying reconnaissance missions over Cuba during the powder-keg days of the 1962 missile crisis. As TIME science writer Jeffrey Kluger once wrote, "It's right that we think about *Challenger* every January 28th. But that does not mean we shouldn't spare a thought for Apollo 1 every January 27 too." ∎